Drawn by Yaya
&
colored by Creasam

Drawn & colored
by
Peggy Sue's Artwork

Global Doodle Gems Volume 7
"The Ultimate international Coloring Book...an Epic Collection from Artists around the World!"

Drawn & colored
by
Rosalien Hanssen

Drawn by Maggie Lin
&
colored by Lilan Chen

Drawn & colored
by
Esther Lafiebre

Drawn & colored
by
Ena Tera Art

Drawn & colored
by
Iben Lykke Højholdt

Drawn & colored
by
Jeanne Burbage

Drawn by Mitchell Manuel
&
colored by Laurence Roucou

Drawn & colored
by
Marieke Raterman-Bos

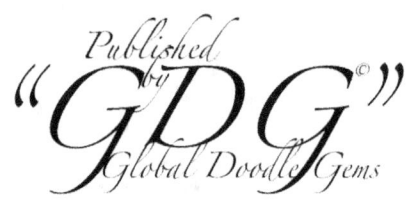

Share your colored versions with us ! We love seeing your results and hearing from you we are social !

The Official FB book page, stay on top of what we have in the works !
www.facebook.com/globaldoodlegems

The Community group, share your colored pages, meet the artists, enjoy exclusive freebies, take part in community Charity books and so much more......
www.facebook.com/groups/globaldoodlegems/

Follow us on Twitter.... @GlobalDoodlegem

We are on Instagram too
@globaldoodlegems for instagram

...and if you are not social like that we have a blog
globaldoodlegems.wordpress.com

Copyright © 2015 Global Doodle Gems

All rights are reserved by Global Doodle Gems.

Duplication of pages for personal use are allowed. You are invited to color the pages then scan/post your coloured versions to social networks, mentioning the book title and author/artist (Global Doodle Gems).

All artwork and images are protected by copyright laws. This book or any portion thereof may not, otherwise, be reproduced and/or distributed or transmitted without the express written permission of the artist/publisher of Global Doodle Gems.

All of us from the Global Doodle Gems wish you a colortastic time and look forward to seeing your wonderful color results online !

Chapter 1
Yaya

Chapter 2
Mitchell Manuel

Chapter 3
Maggie Lin

Chapter 4
Iben Lykke Højholdt

Chapter 5
Jeanne Burbage

Chapter 6
Marieke Raterman-Bos

Chapter 7
Rosalien Hanssen

Chapter 8
Ena Tera Art

Chapter 9
Esther Lafiebre

Chapter 10
Peggy Sue's Artwork

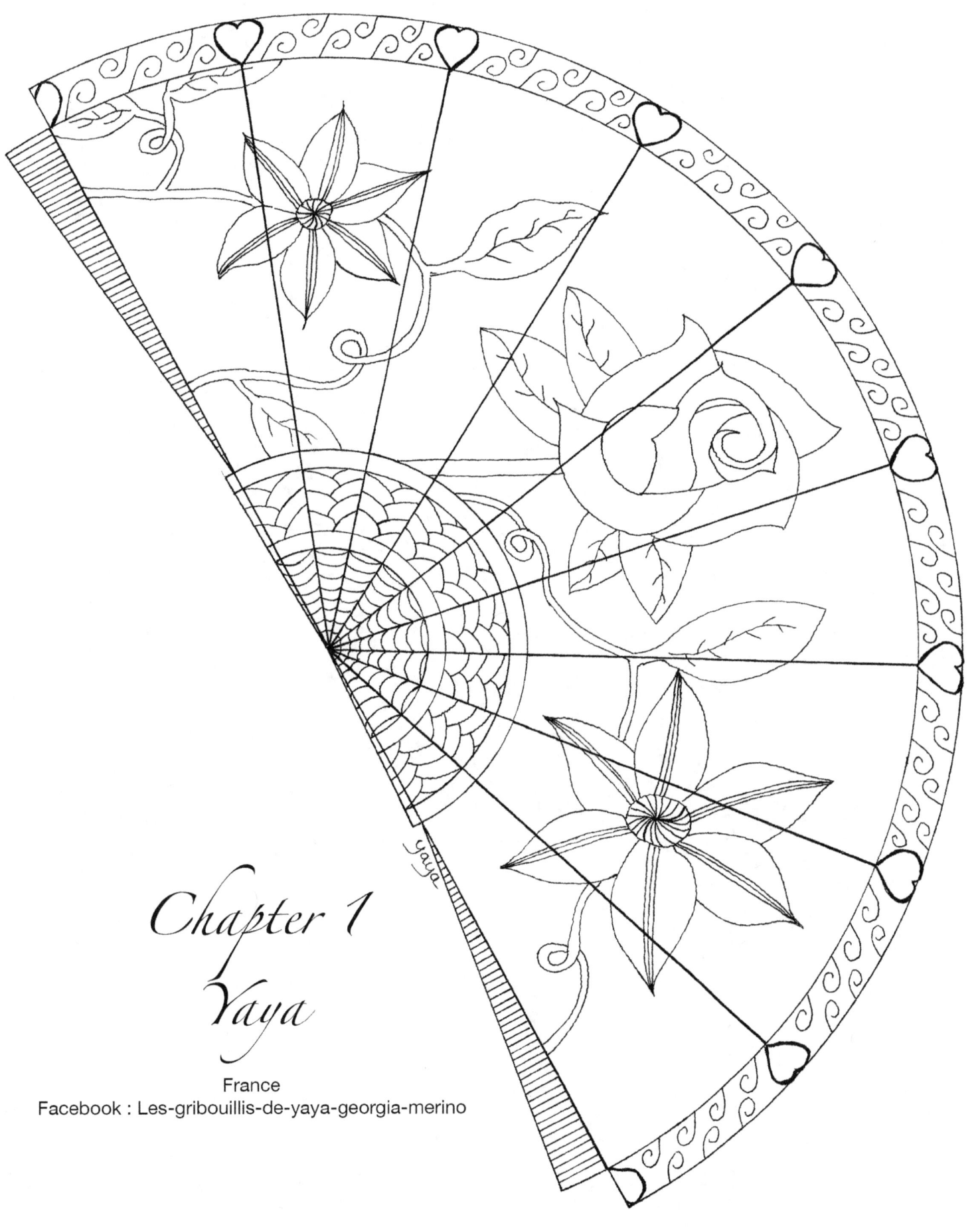

Chapter 1
Yaya

France
Facebook : Les-gribouillis-de-yaya-georgia-merino

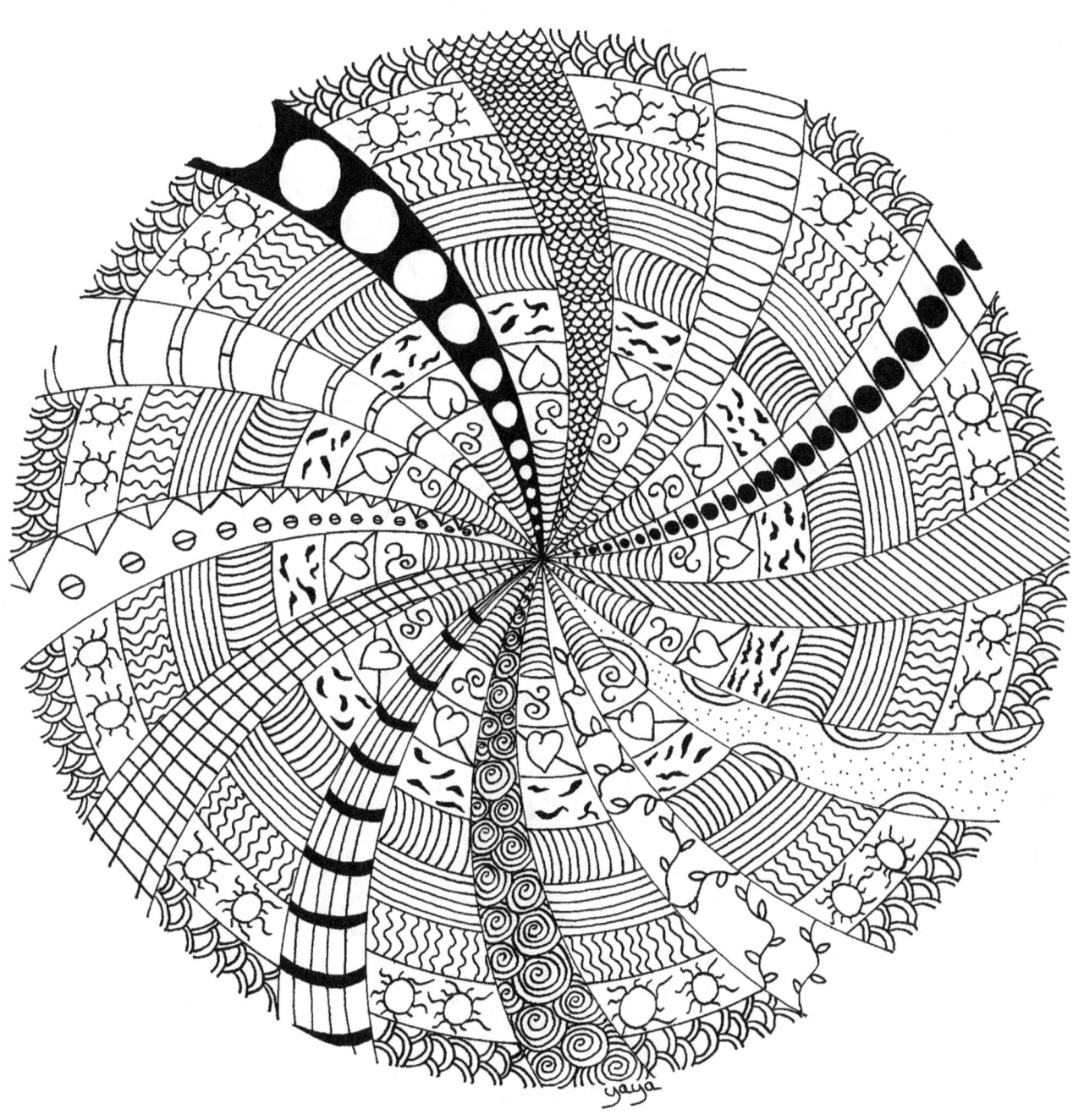

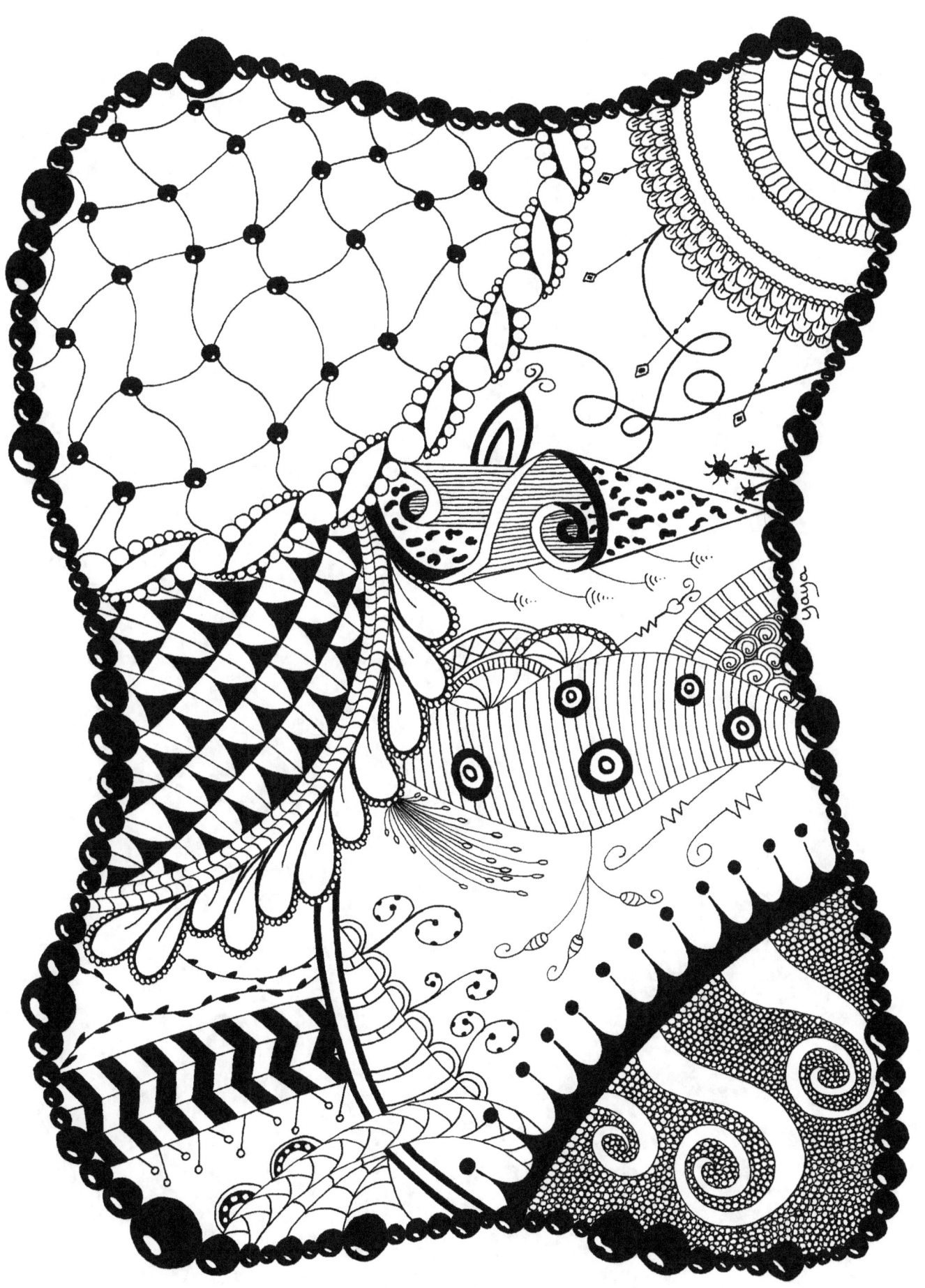

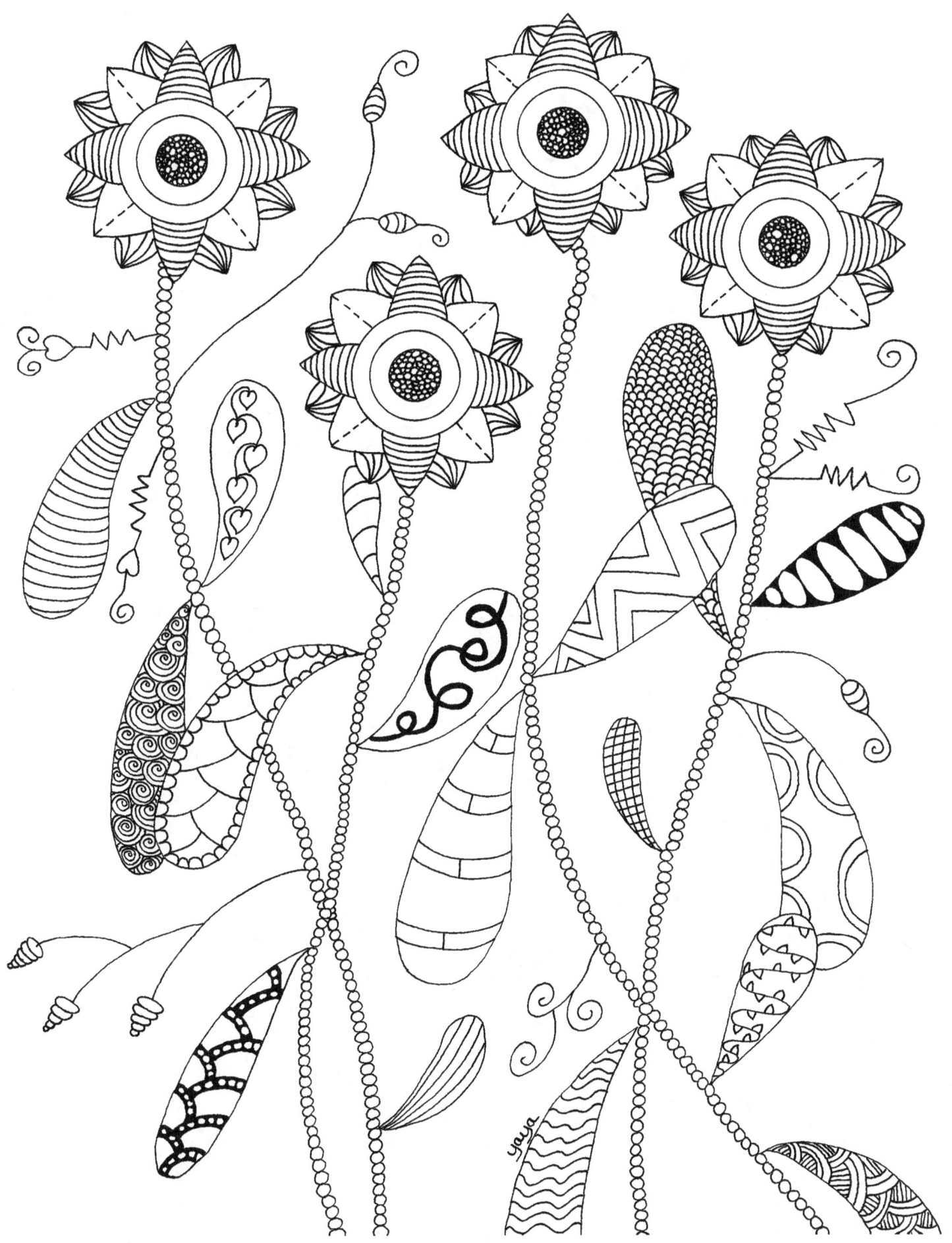

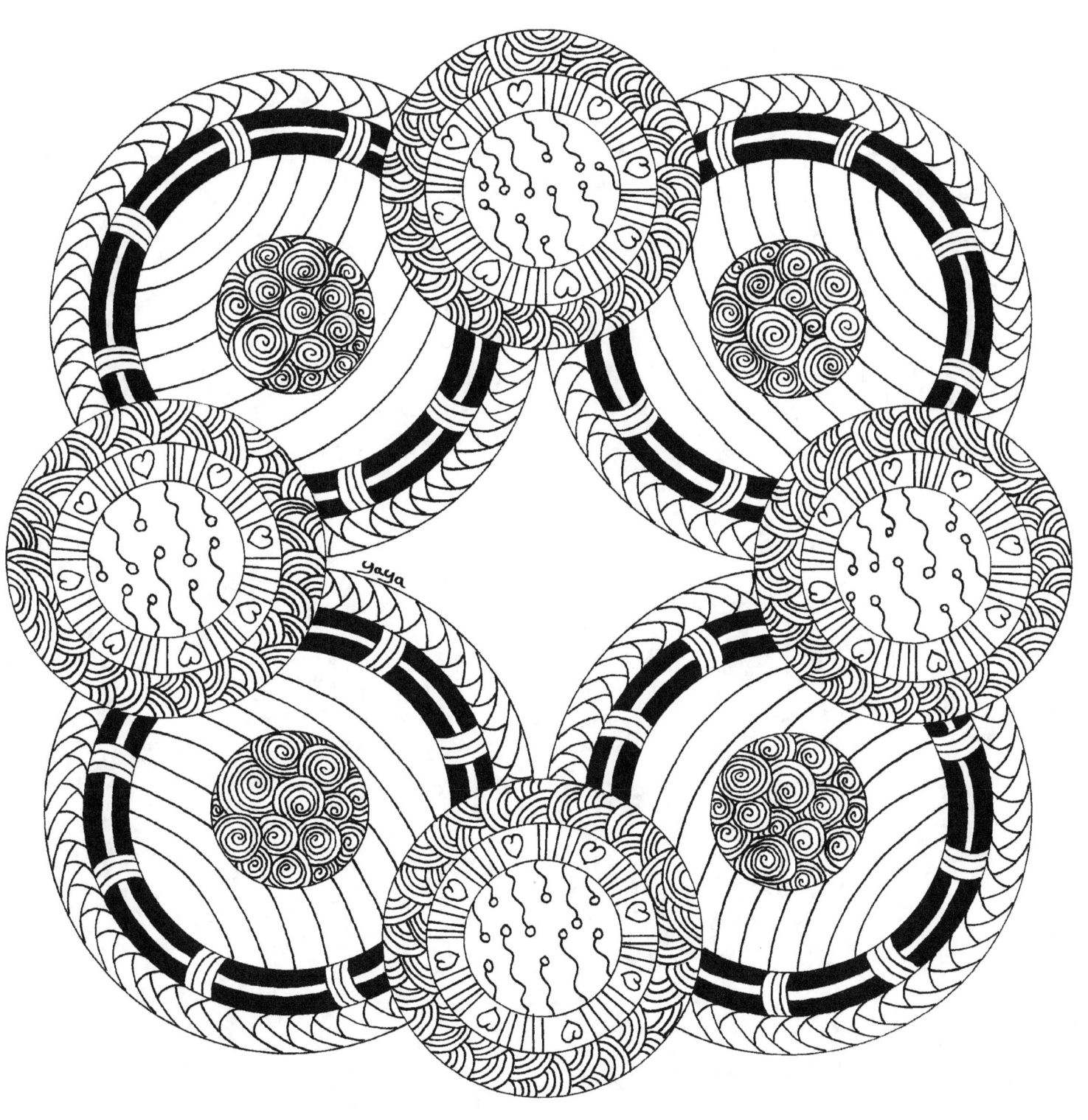

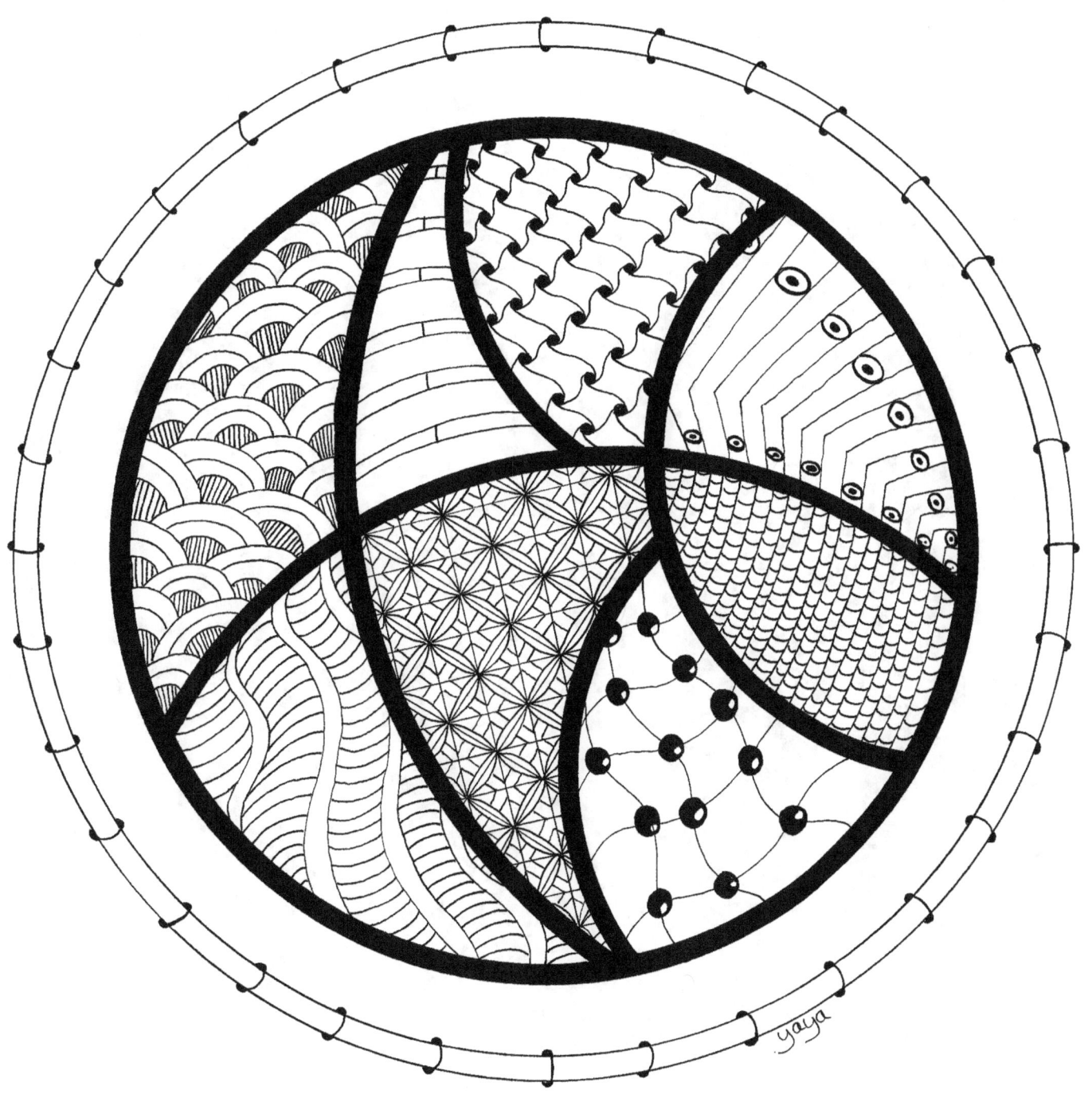

Chapter 2
Mitchell Manuel

New Zealand AKA Aotearoa

http://www.maoriart.org.nz/ngati-apai-ngati-toorangati-taraare-mitch-manuel-p-539.html

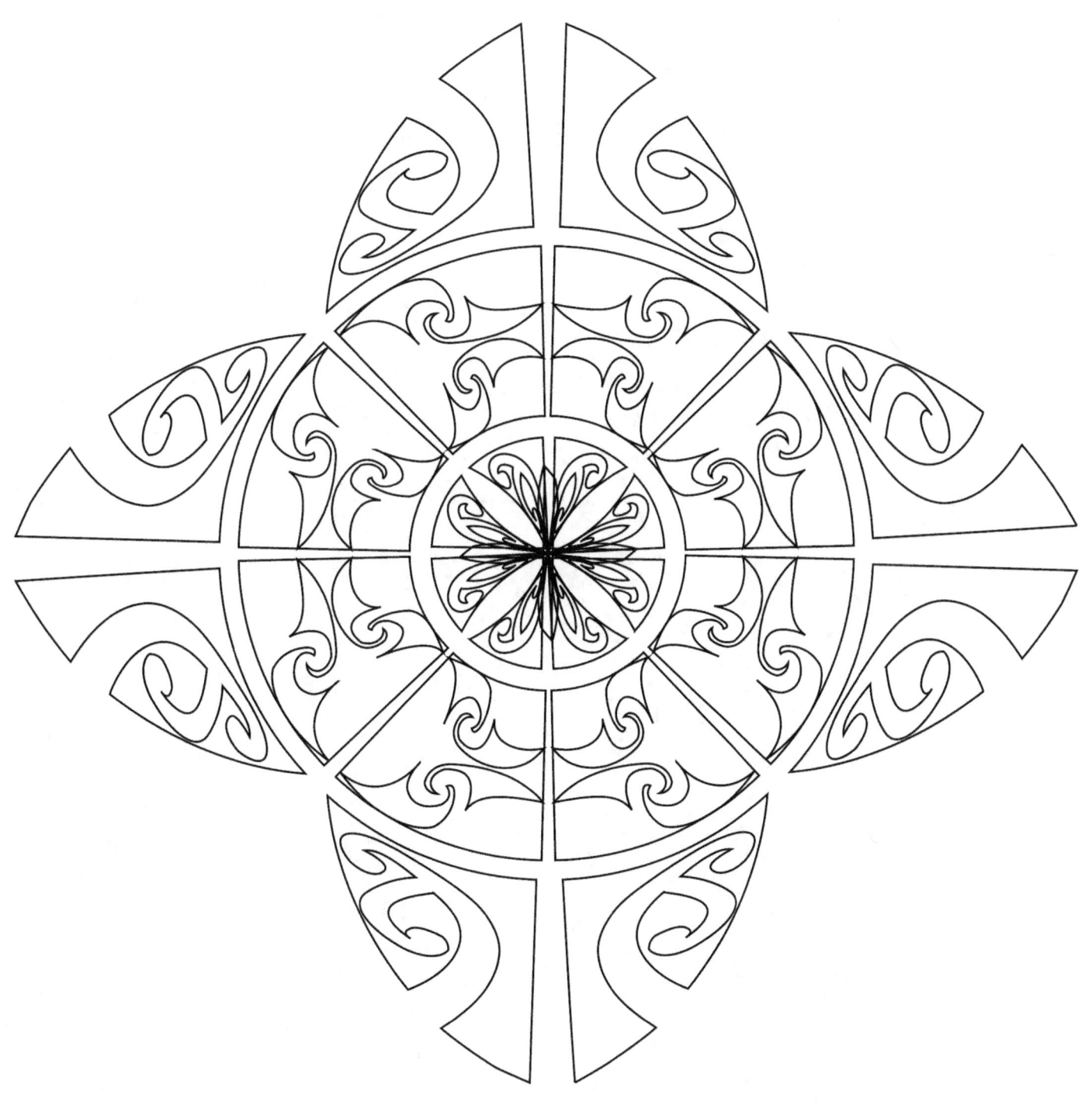

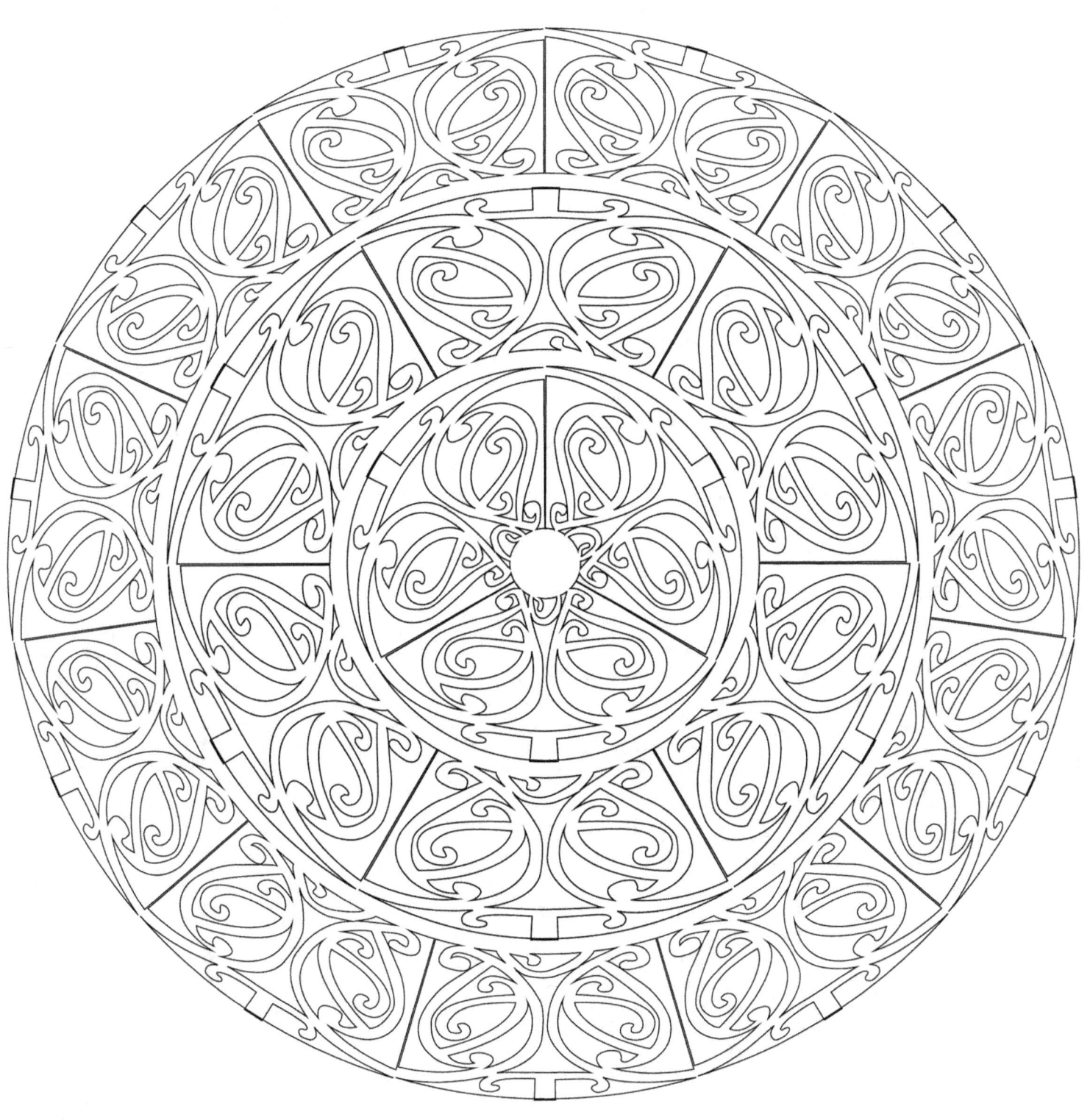

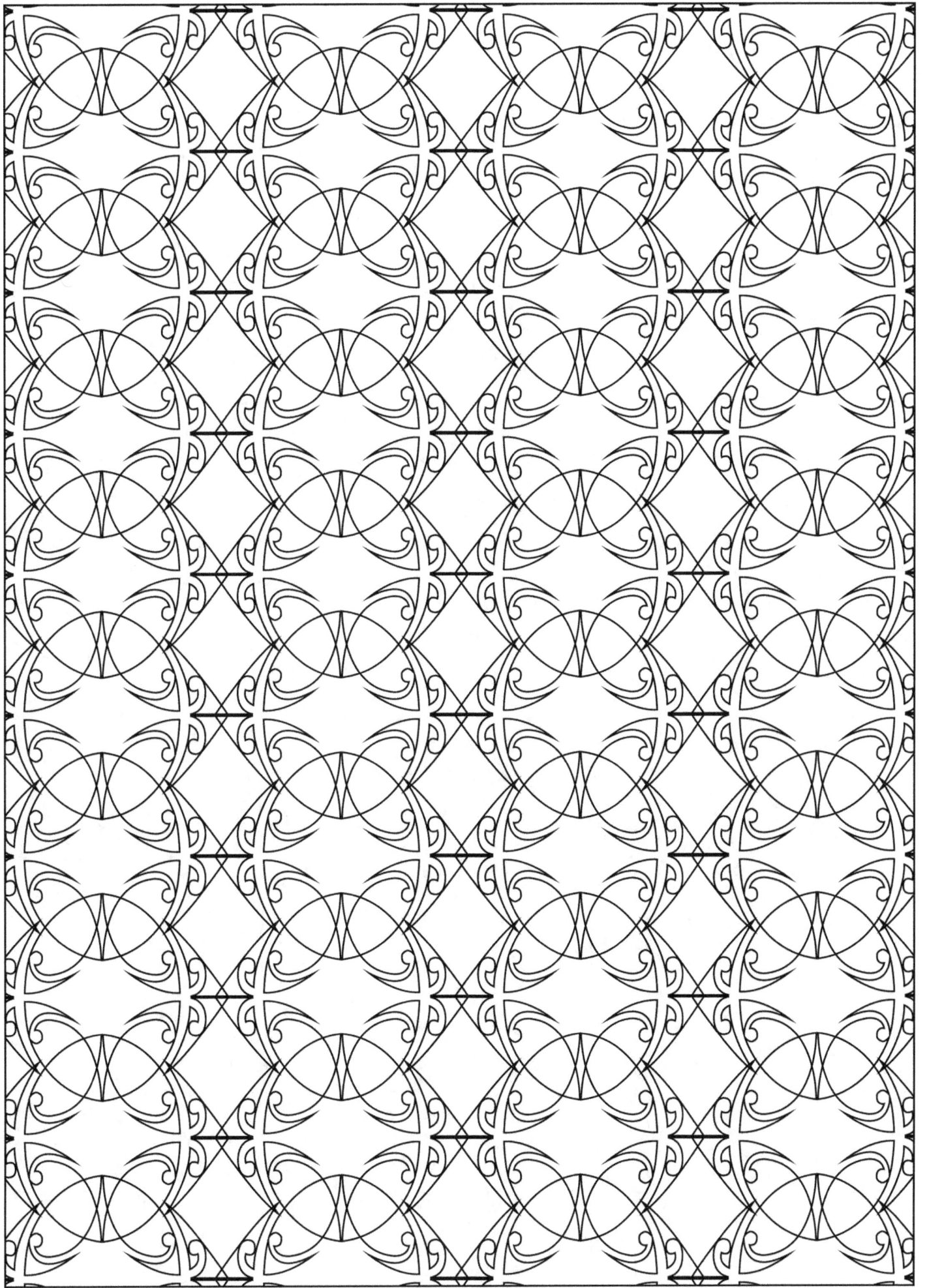

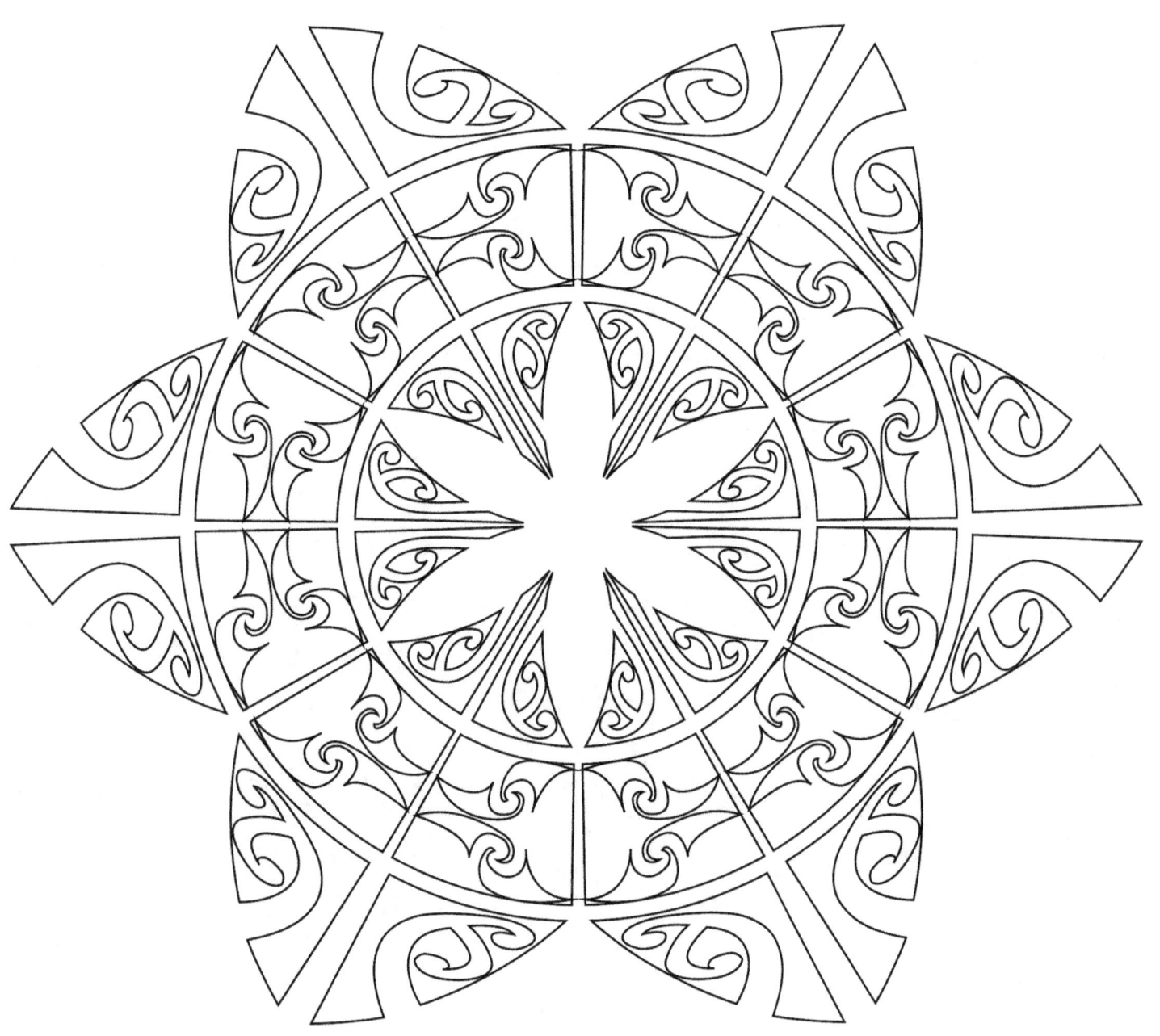

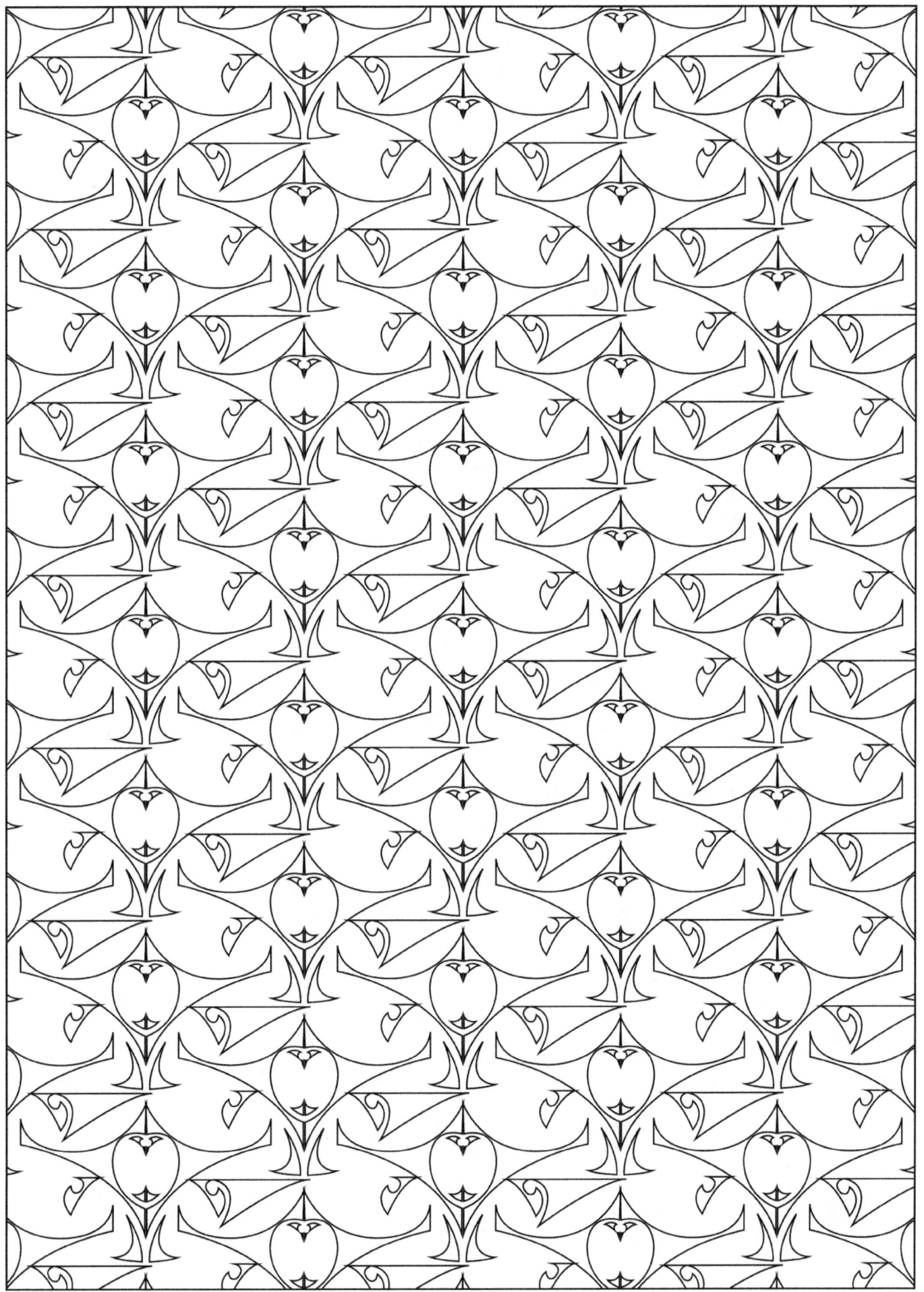

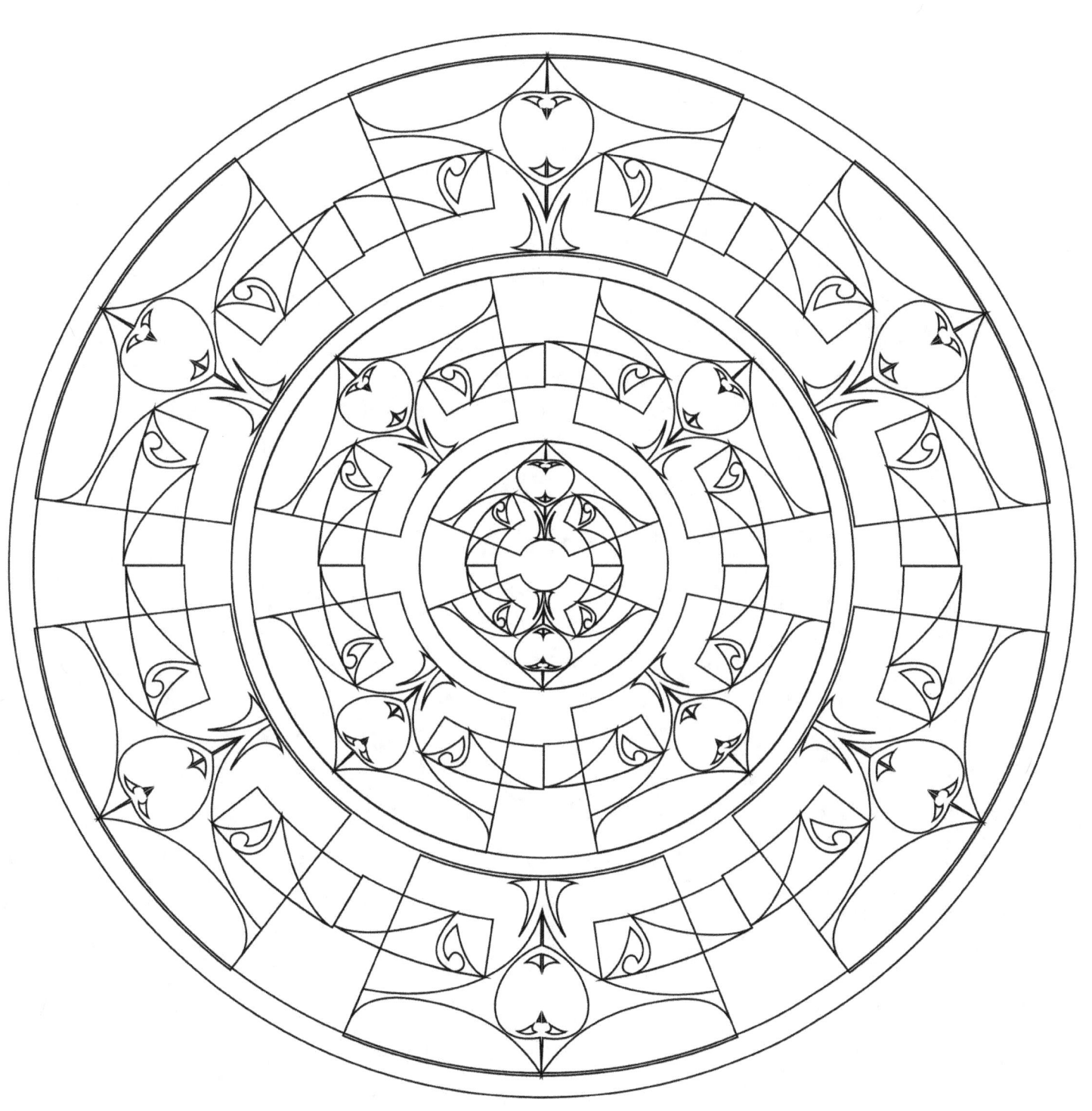

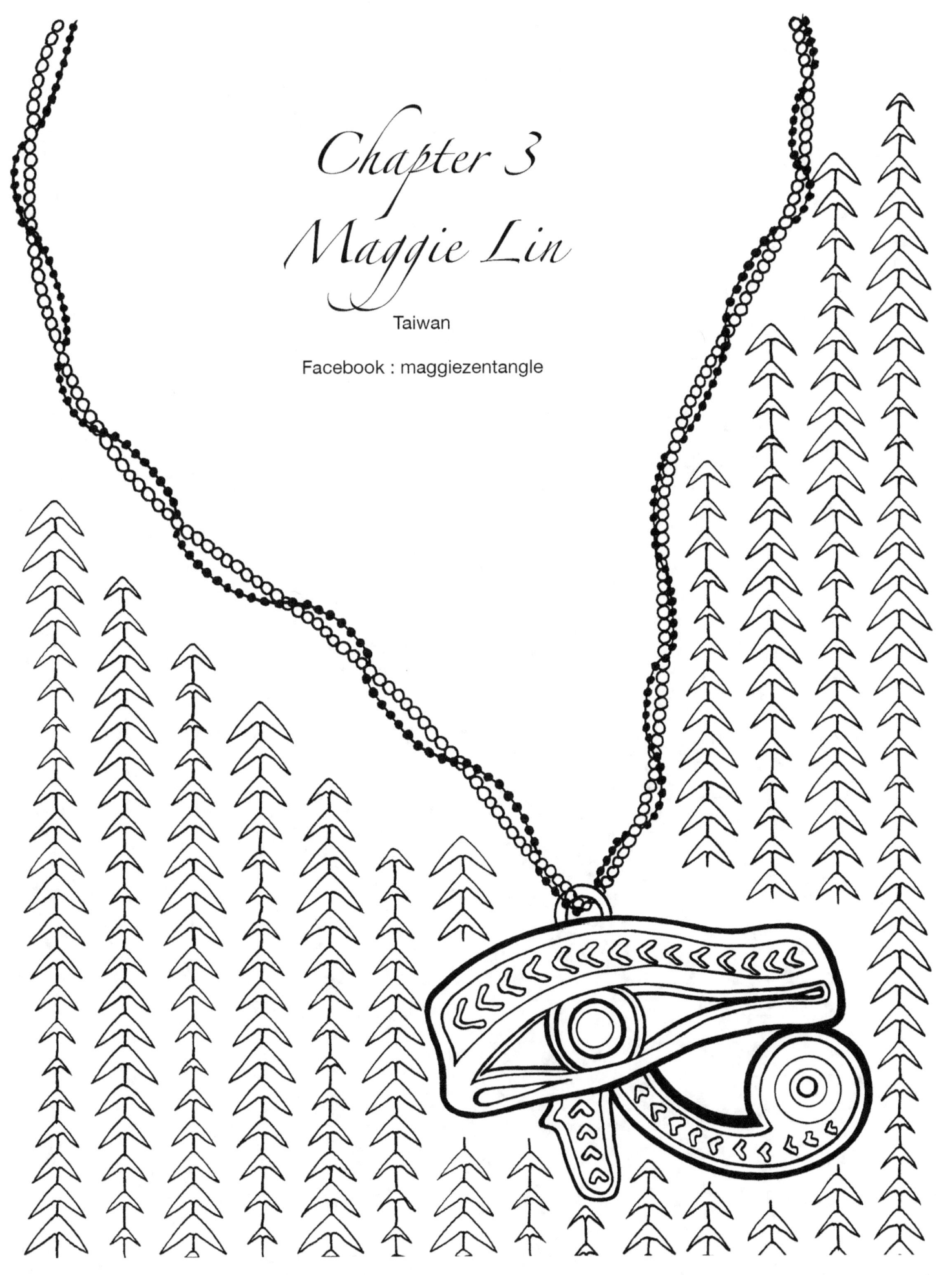

Chapter 3
Maggie Lin

Taiwan

Facebook : maggiezentangle

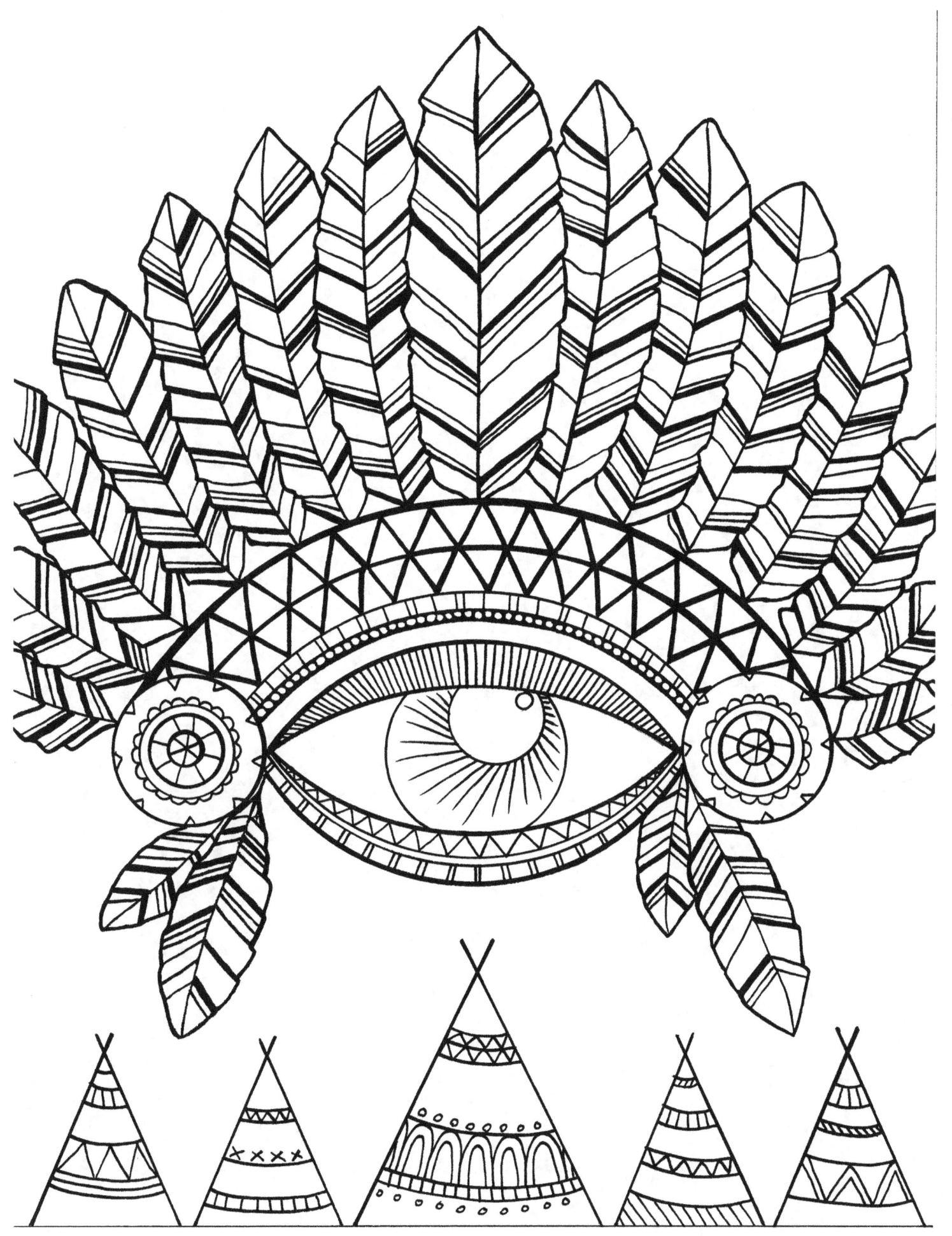

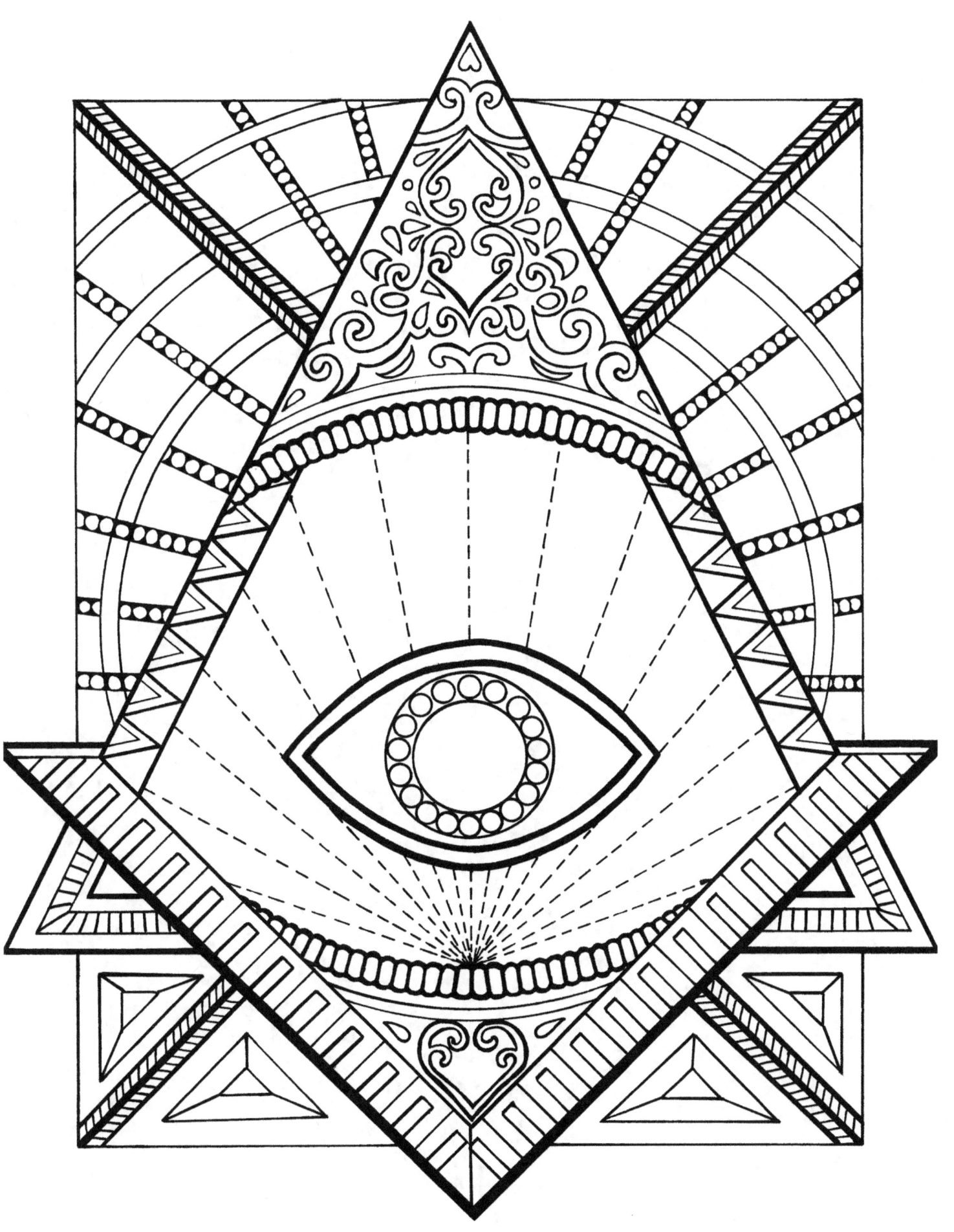

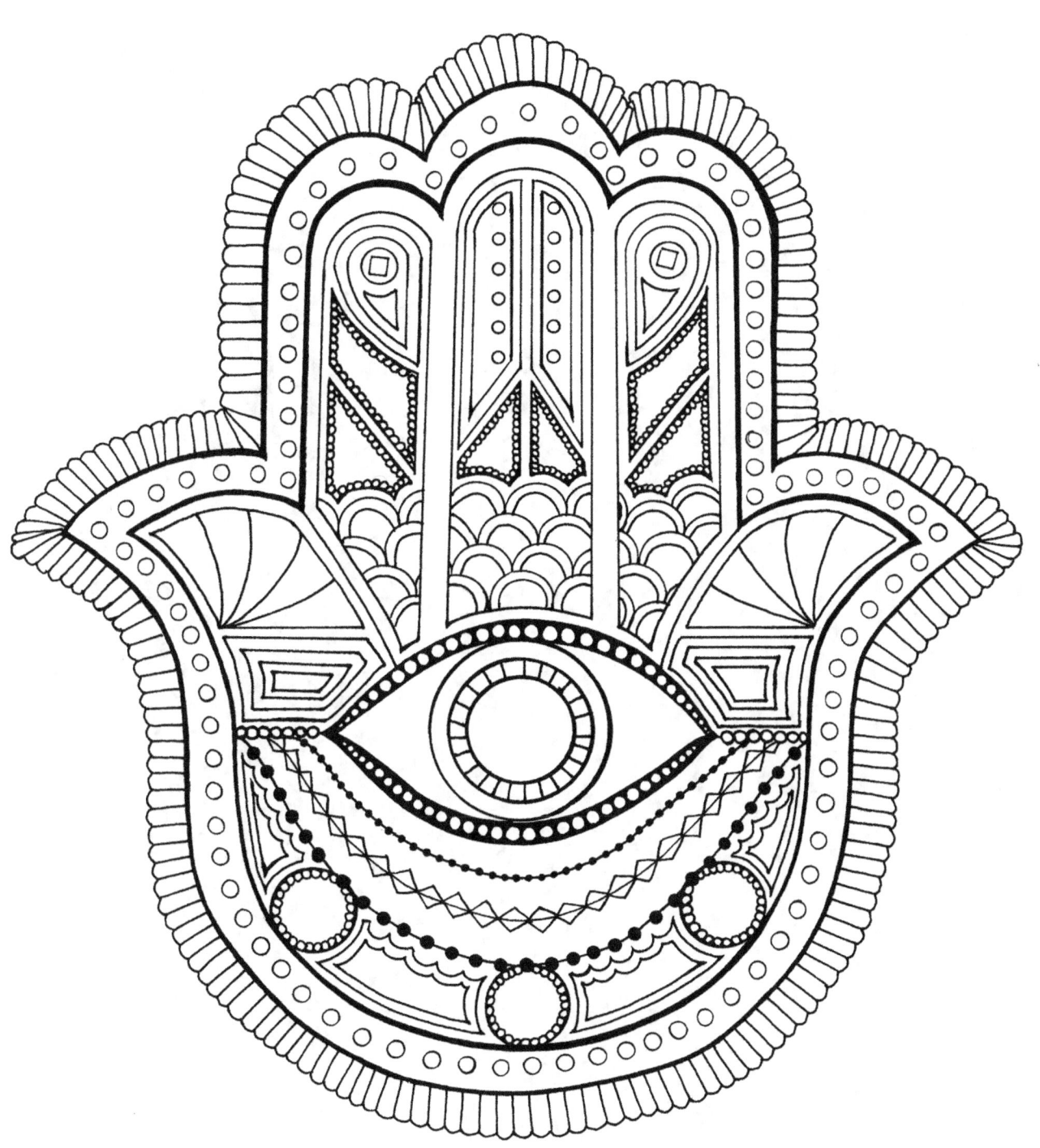

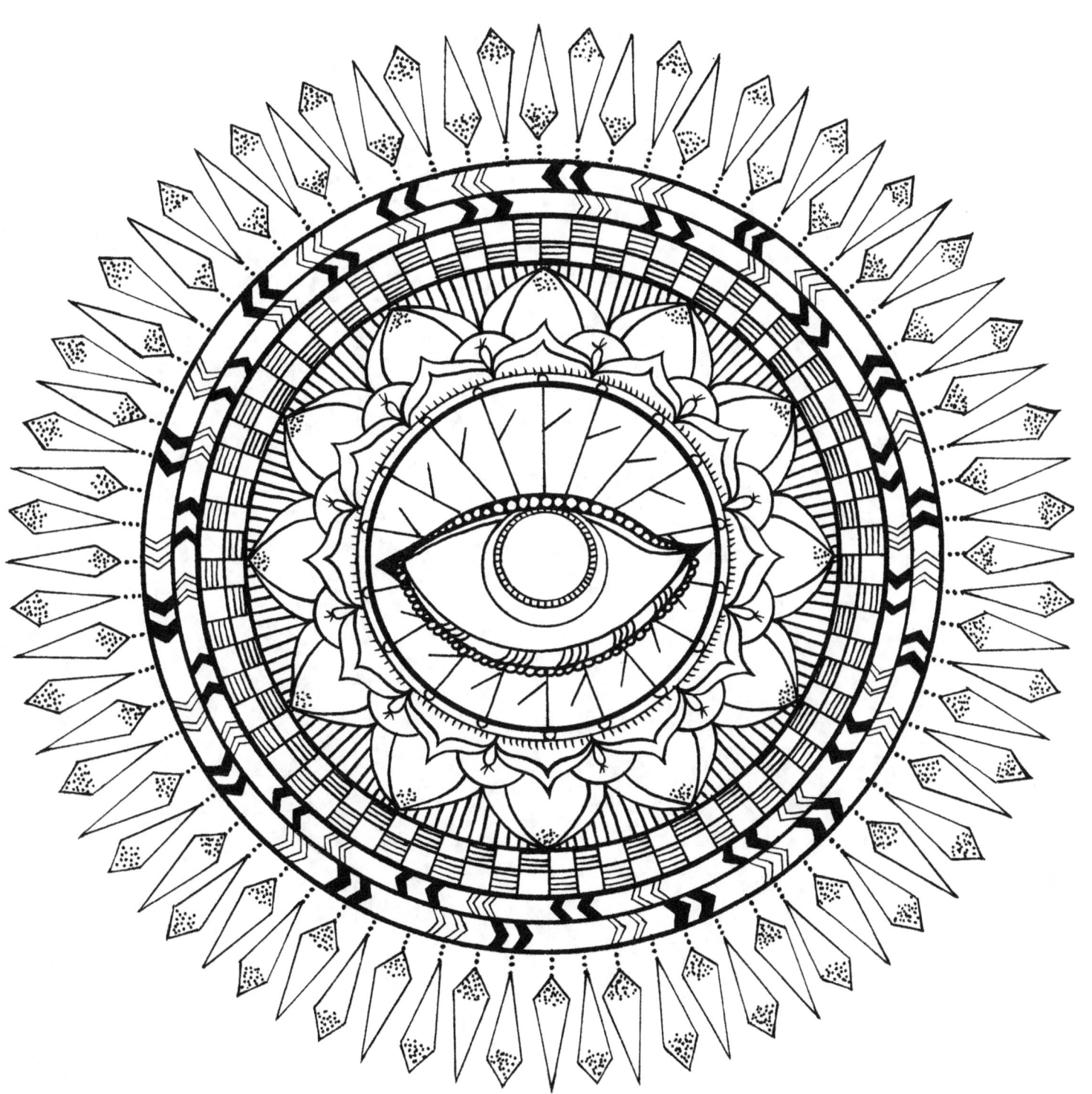

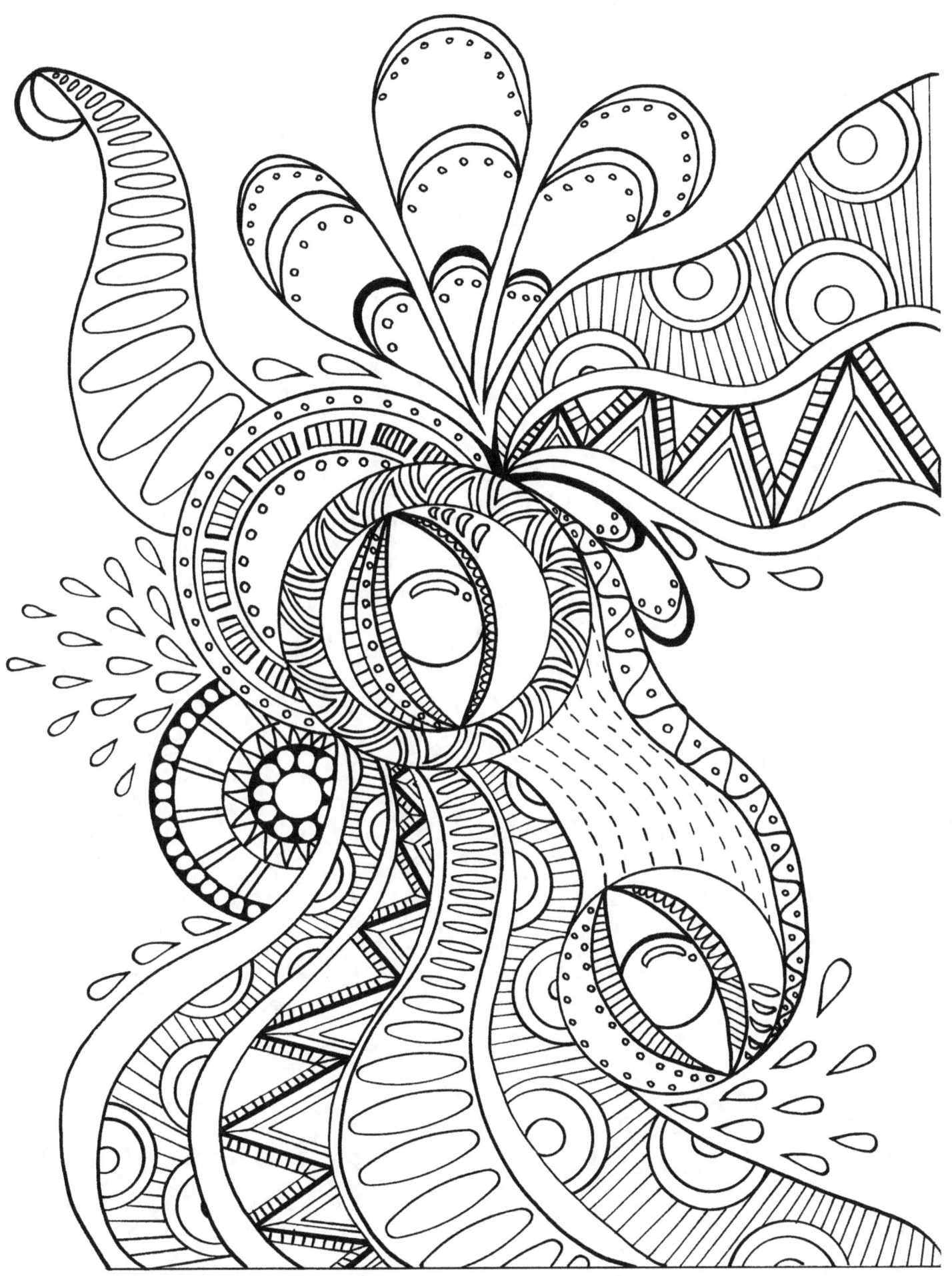

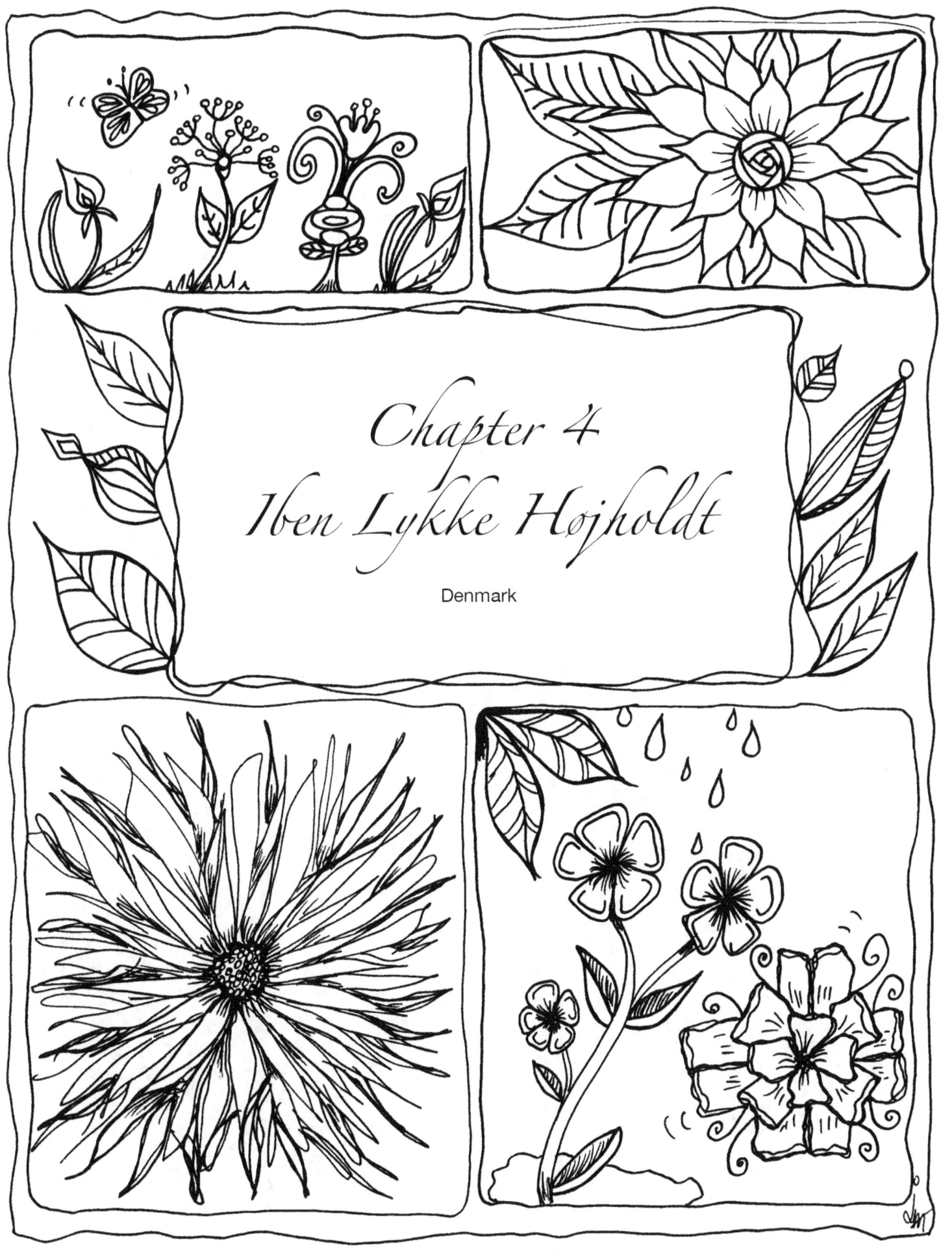

Chapter 4
Iben Lykke Højholdt

Denmark

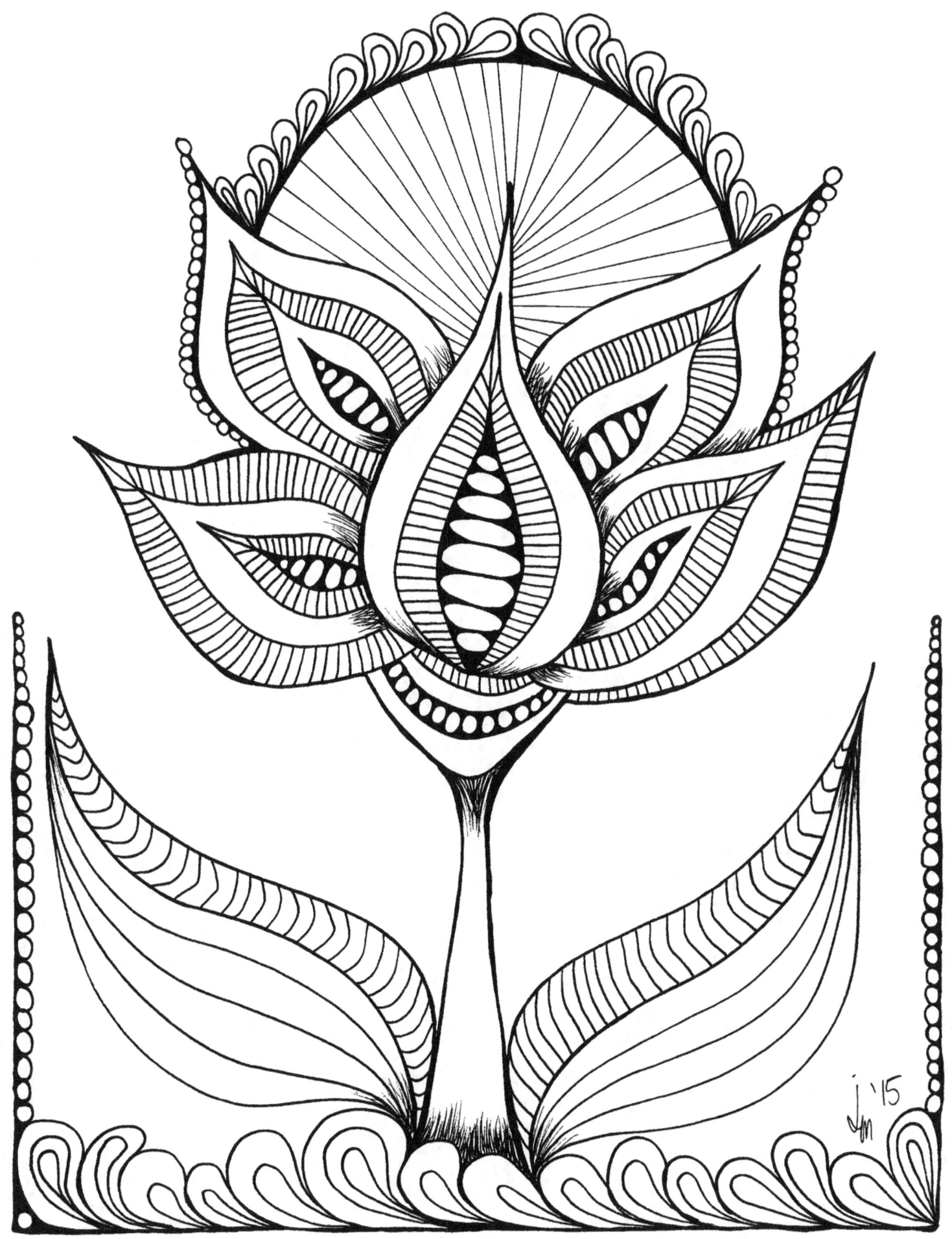

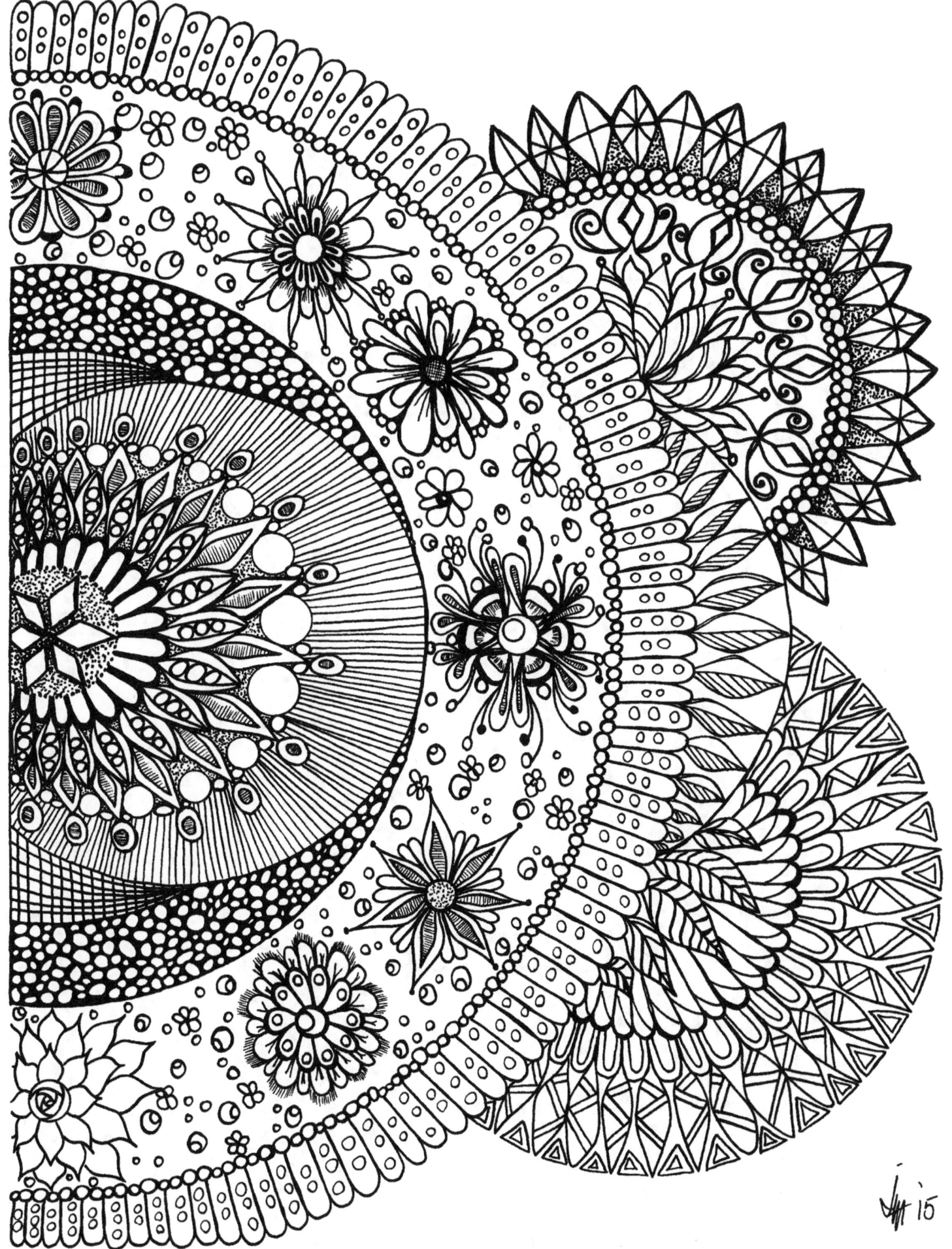

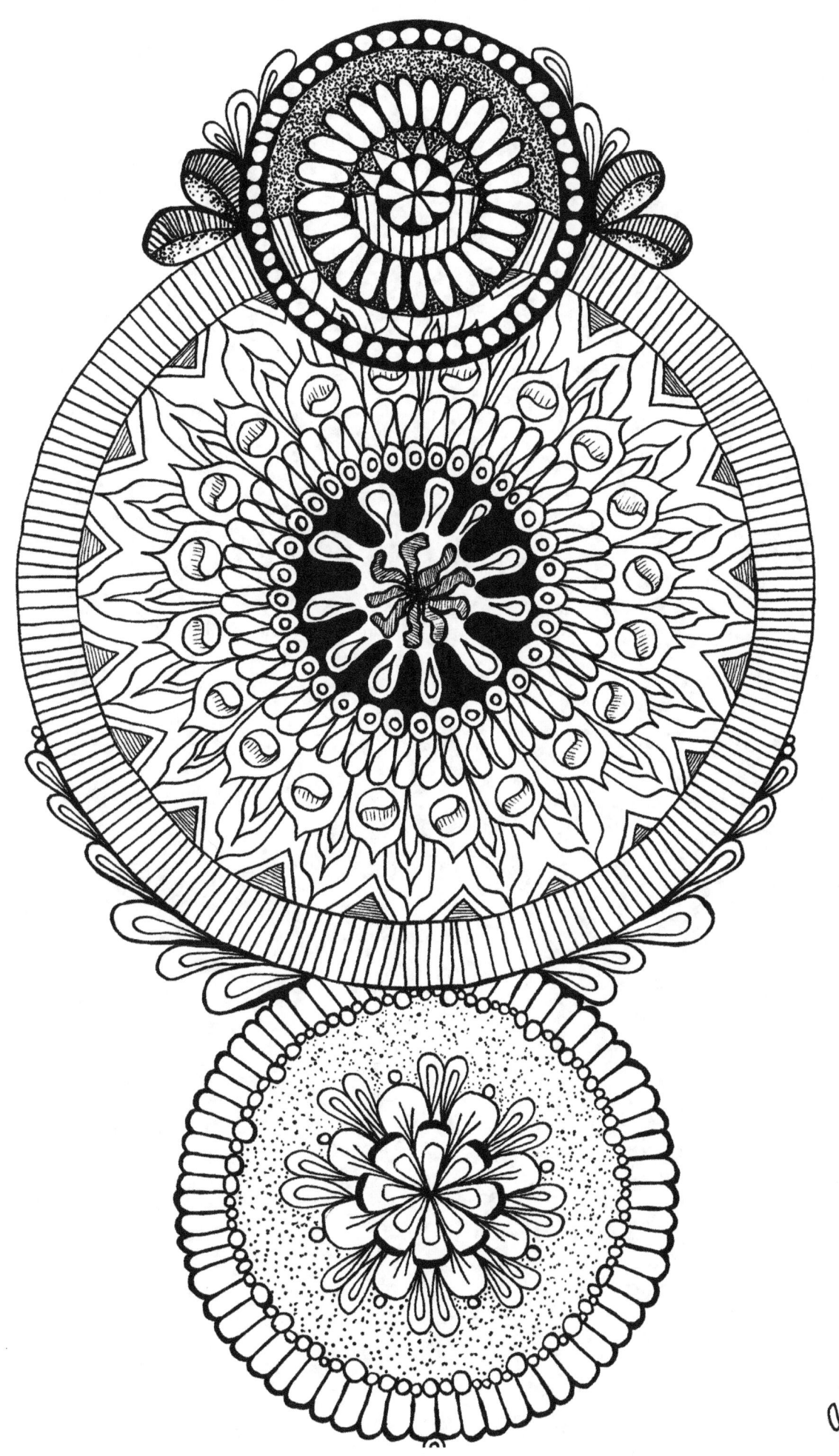

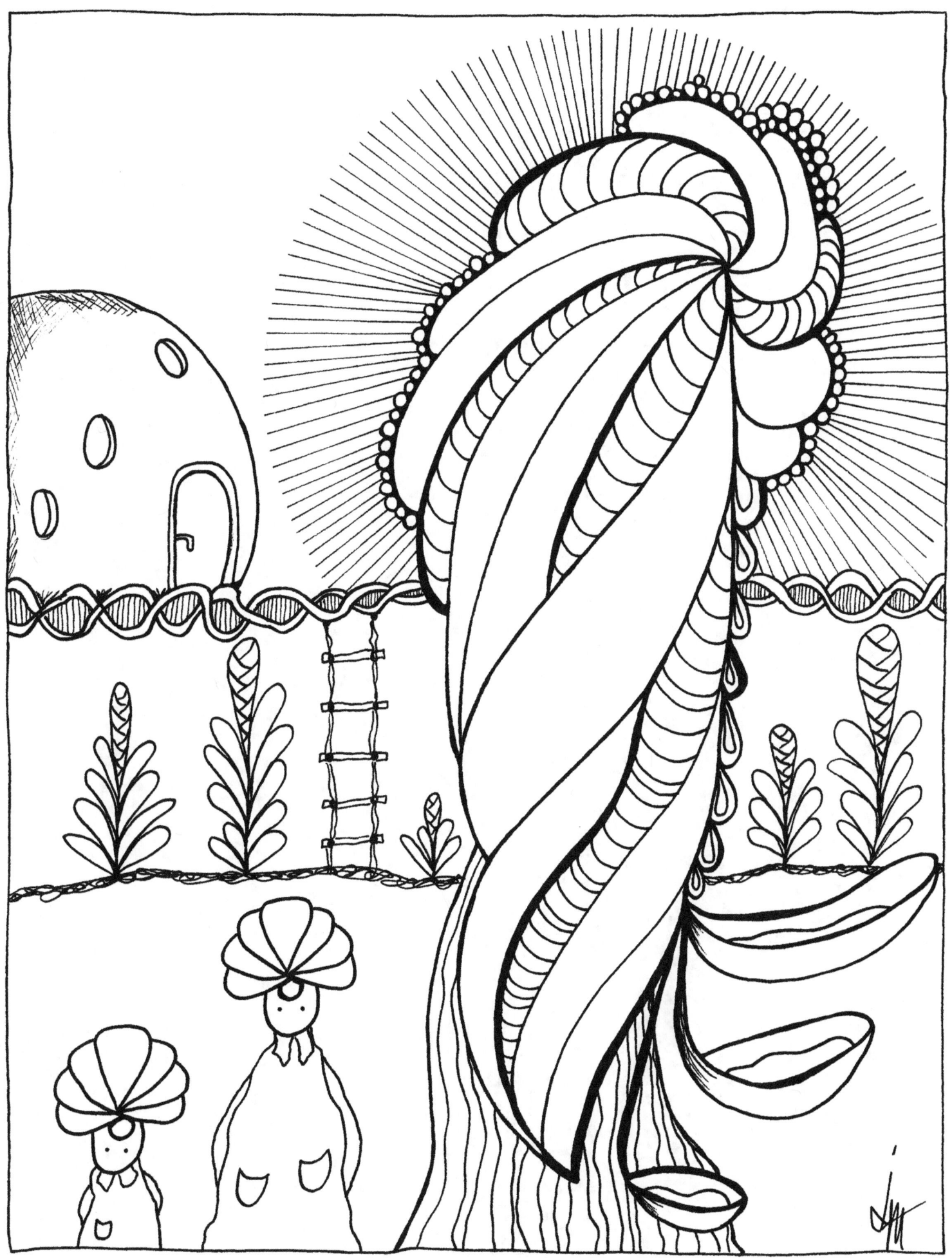

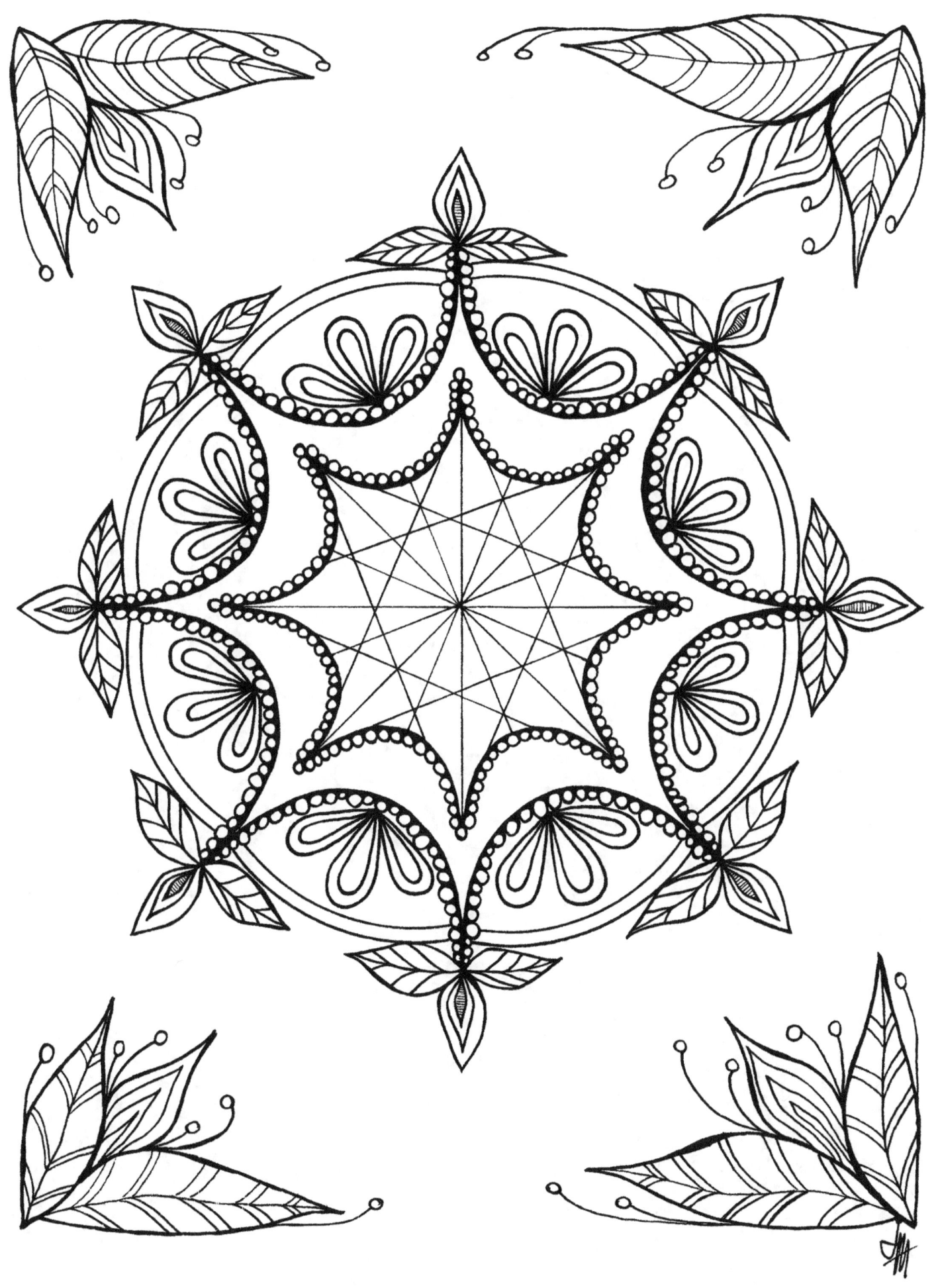

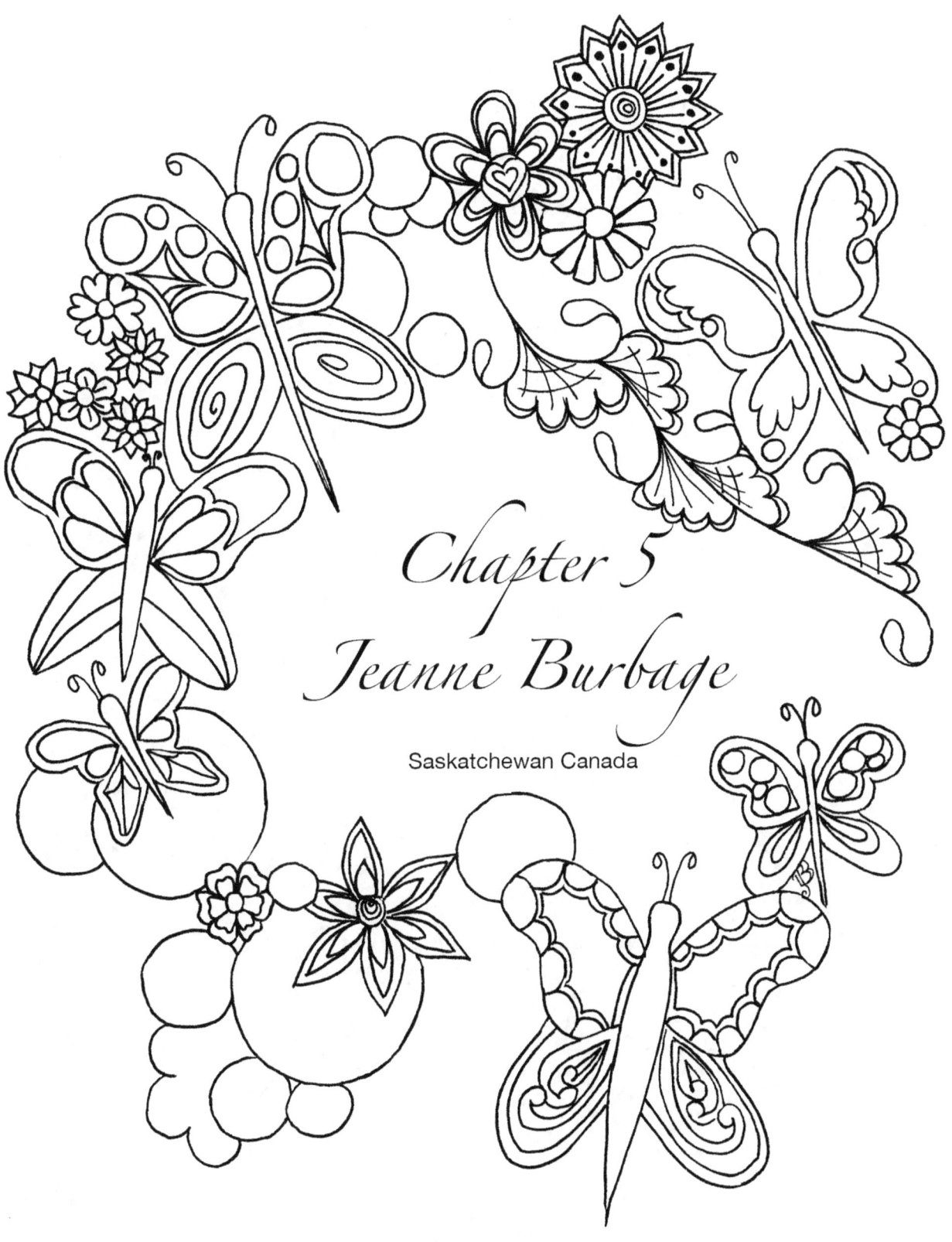

Chapter 5
Jeanne Burbage
Saskatchewan Canada

http://www.zentasticlinesanddesigns.ca/
http://www.zazzle.ca/zenimaginarium
http://driverworks.ca/The-Zenimaginarium-Garden-Coloring-Book.php
Facebook : Zenimaginarium
Facebook Group : thisnthatlinesanddesigns
Etsy shop : zenimaginarium

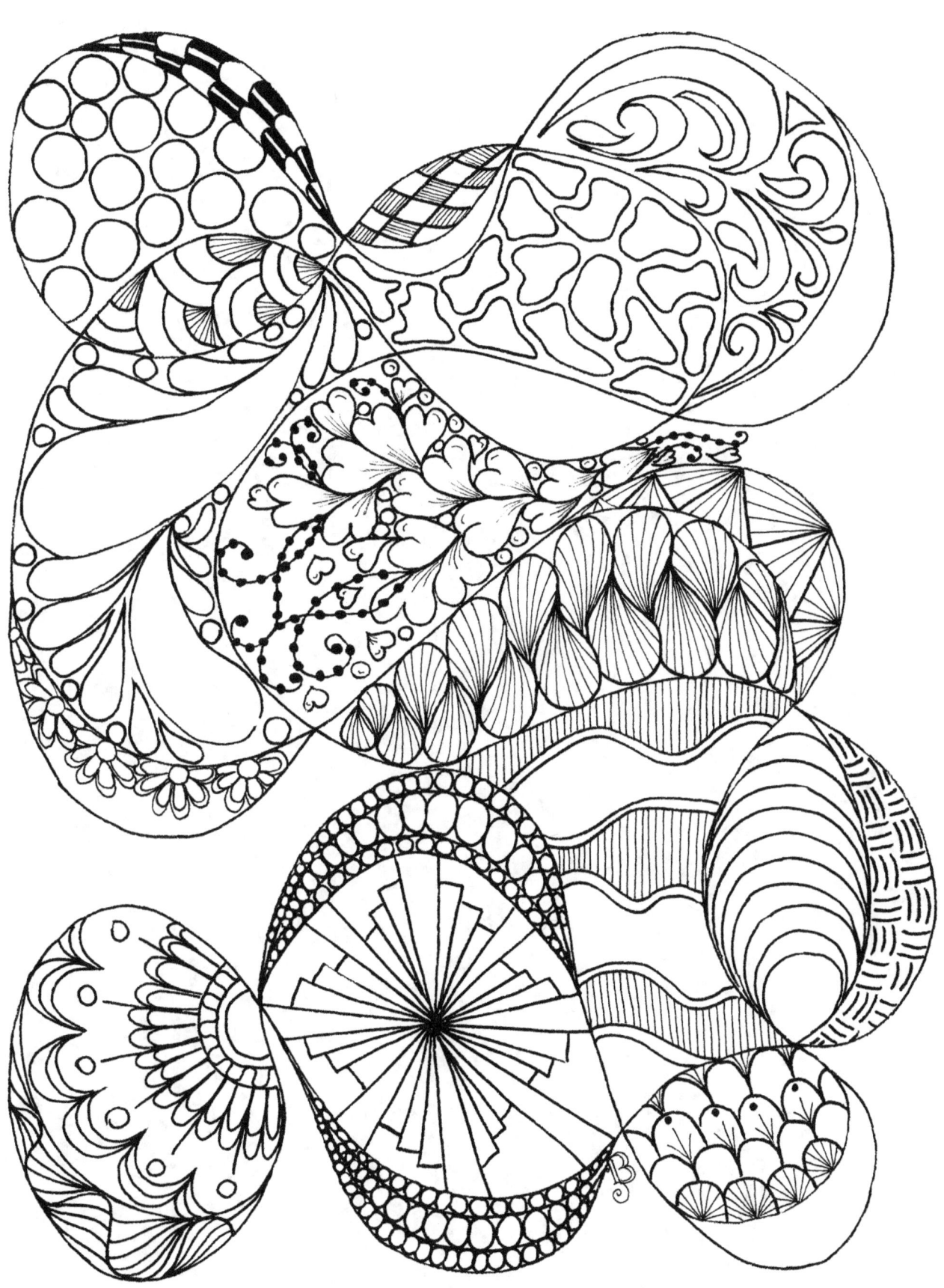

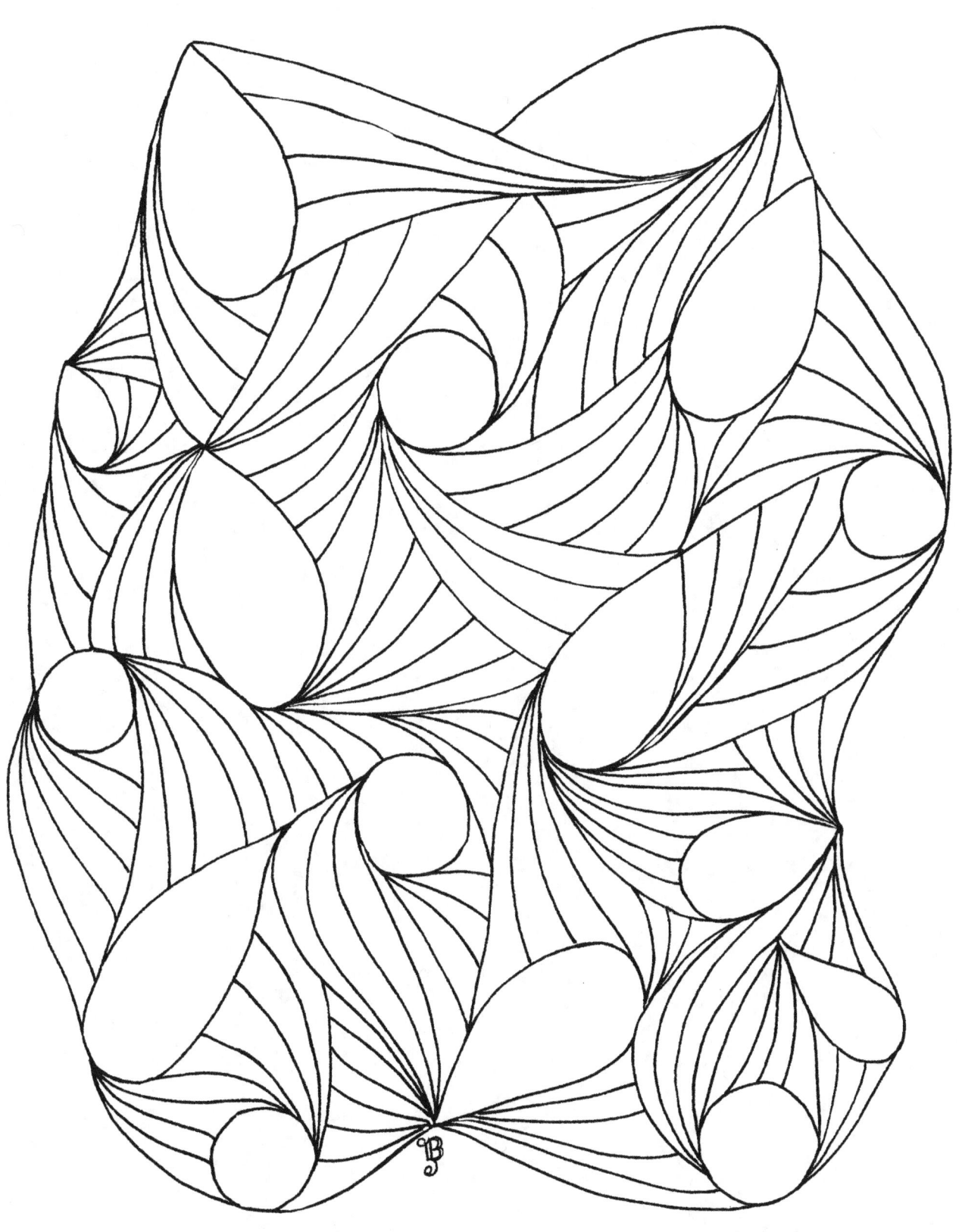

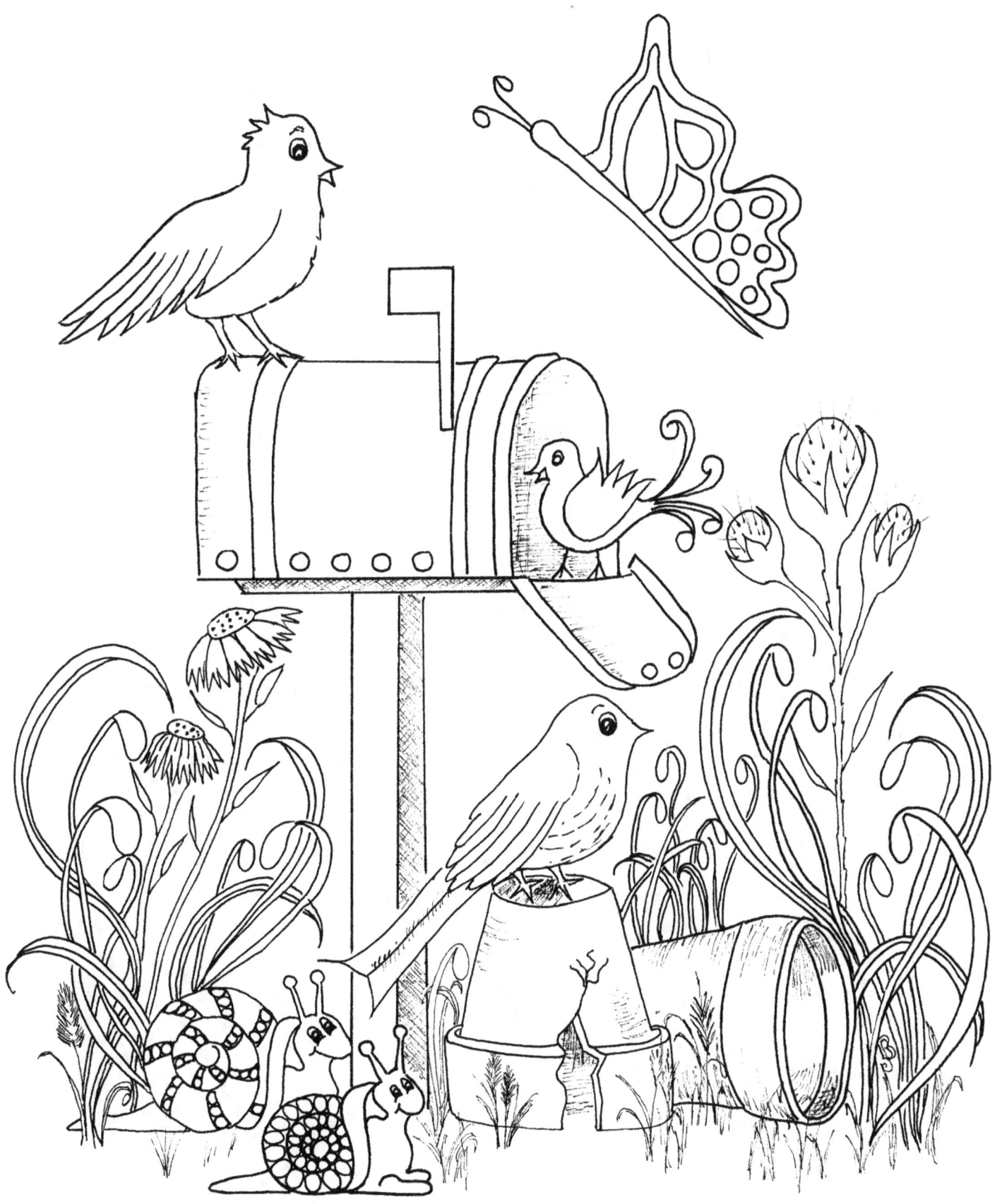

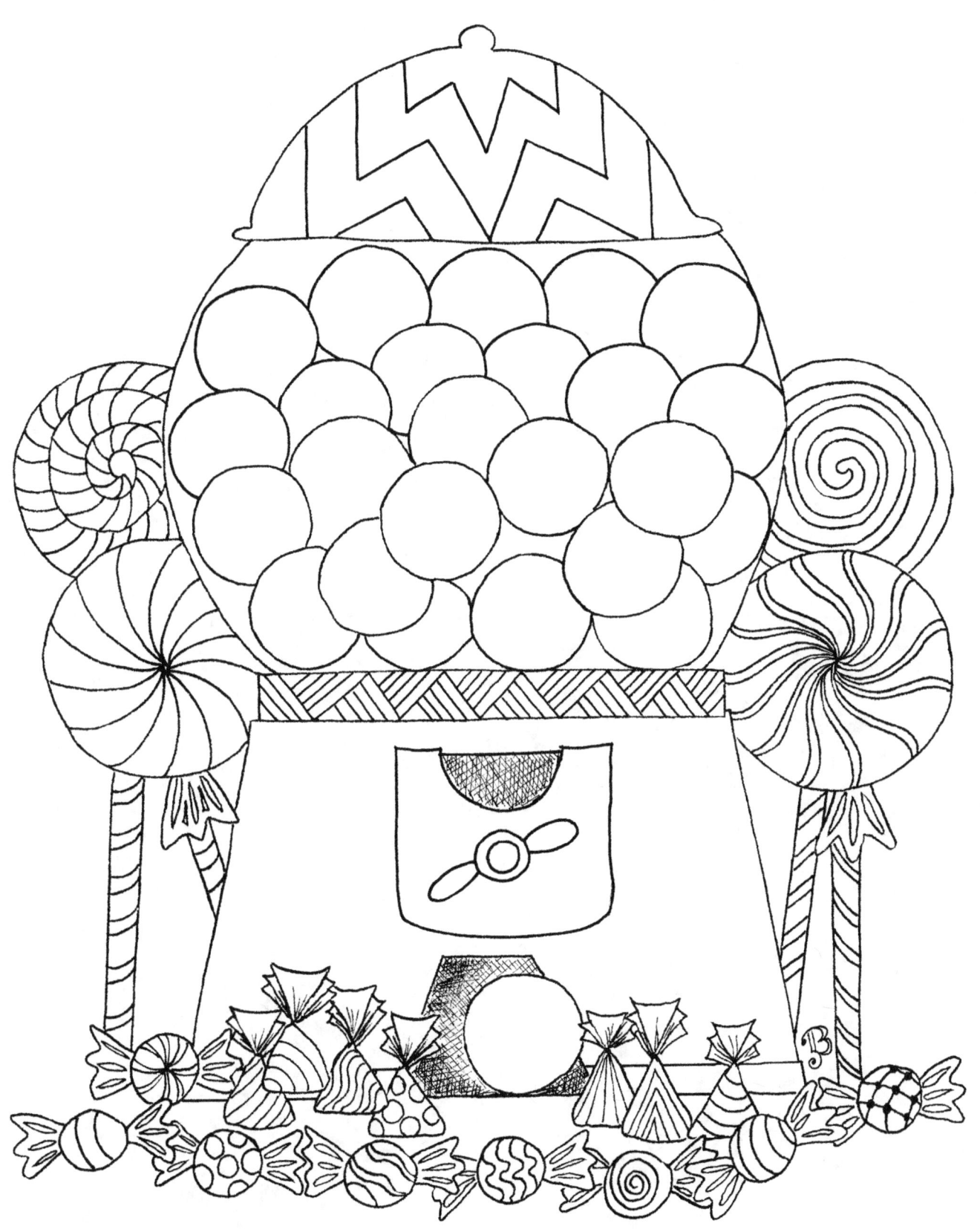

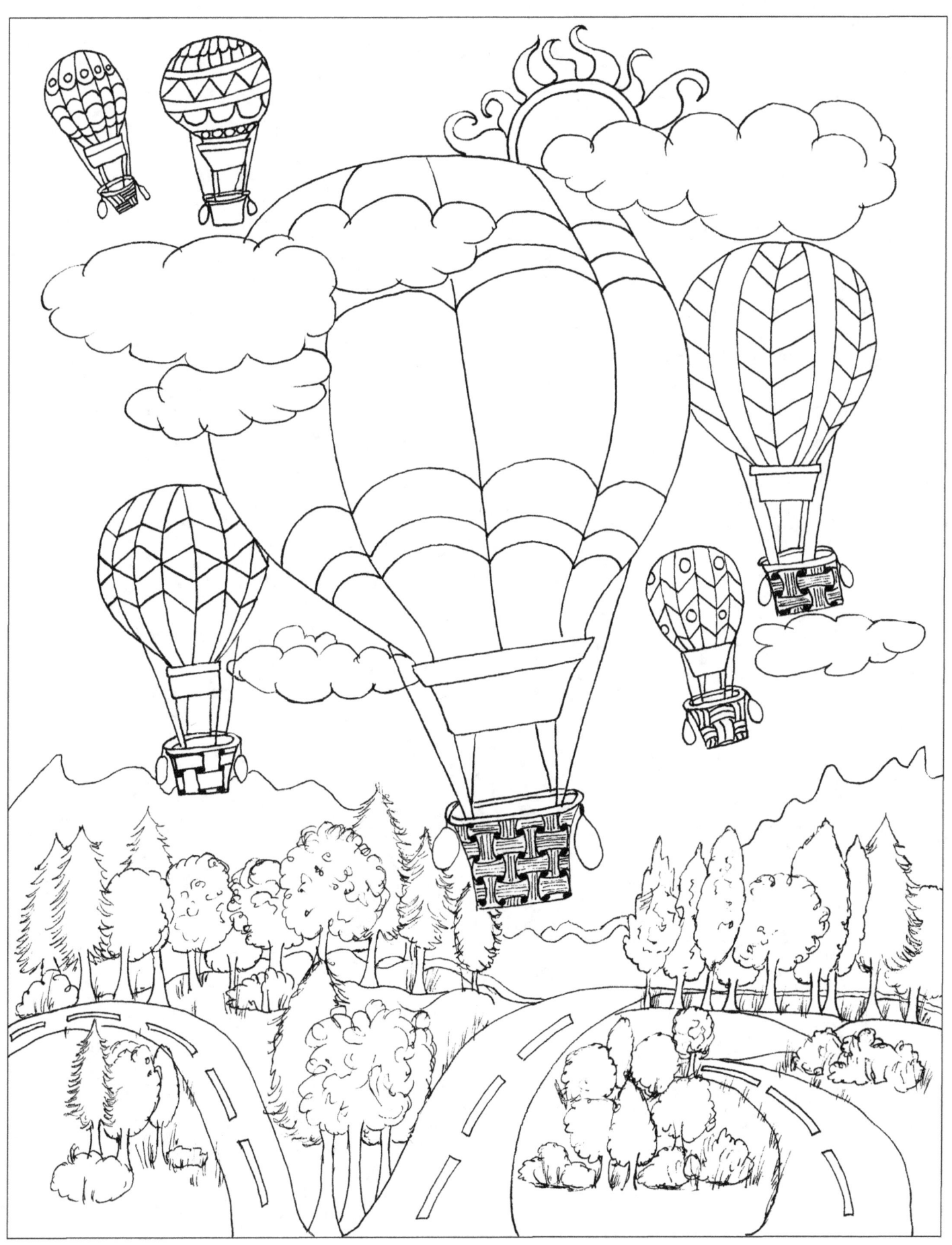

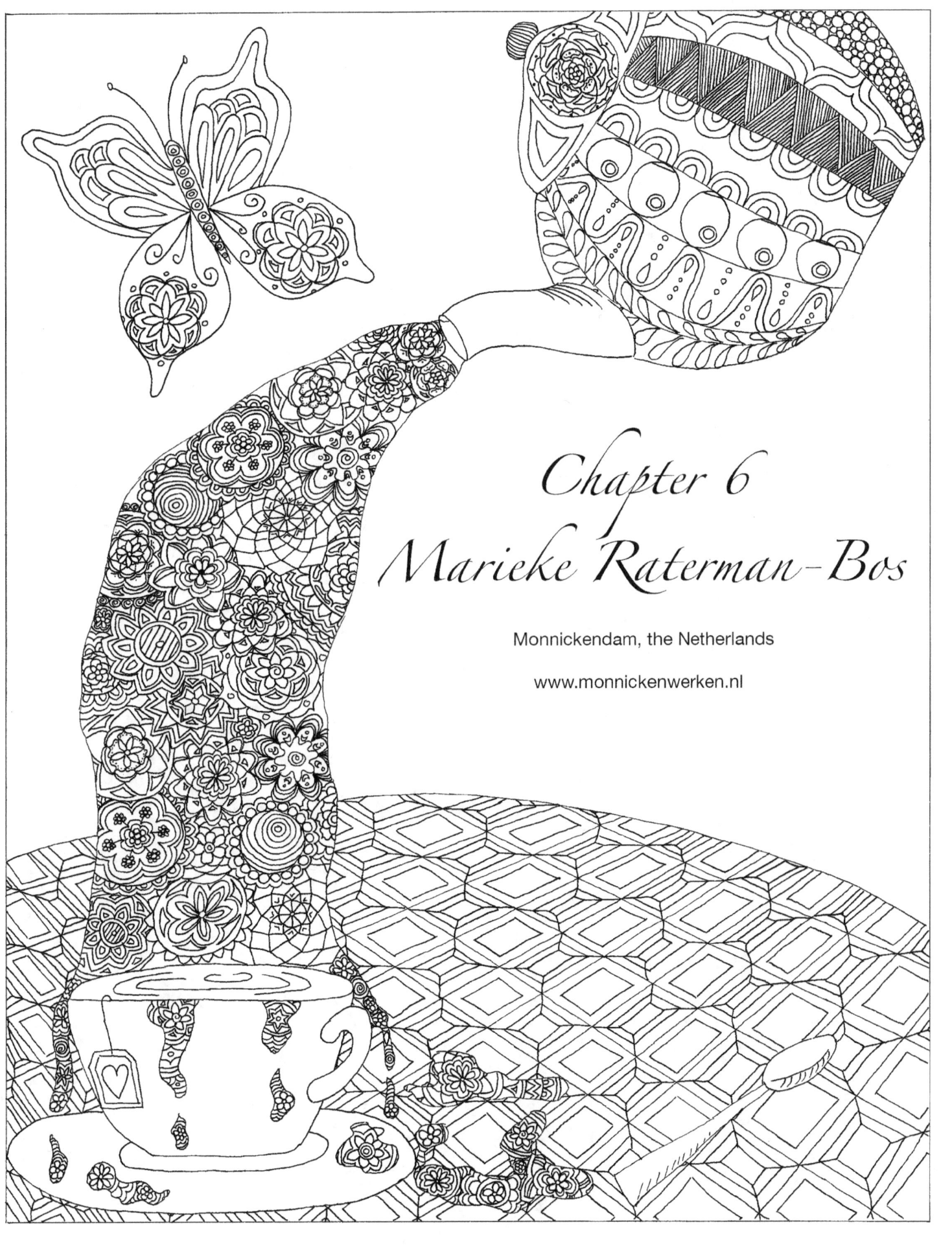

Chapter 6
Marieke Raterman-Bos

Monnickendam, the Netherlands

www.monnickenwerken.nl

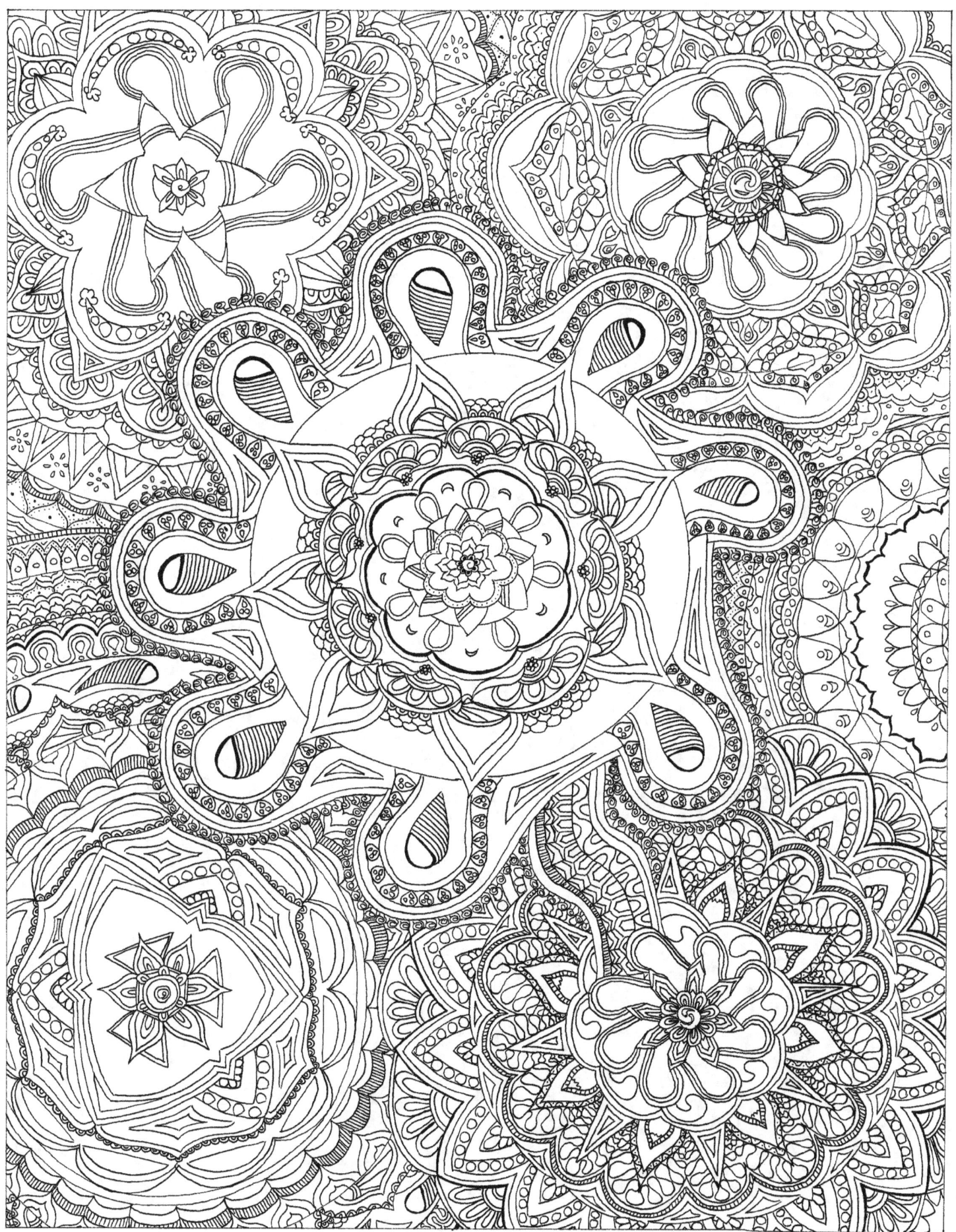

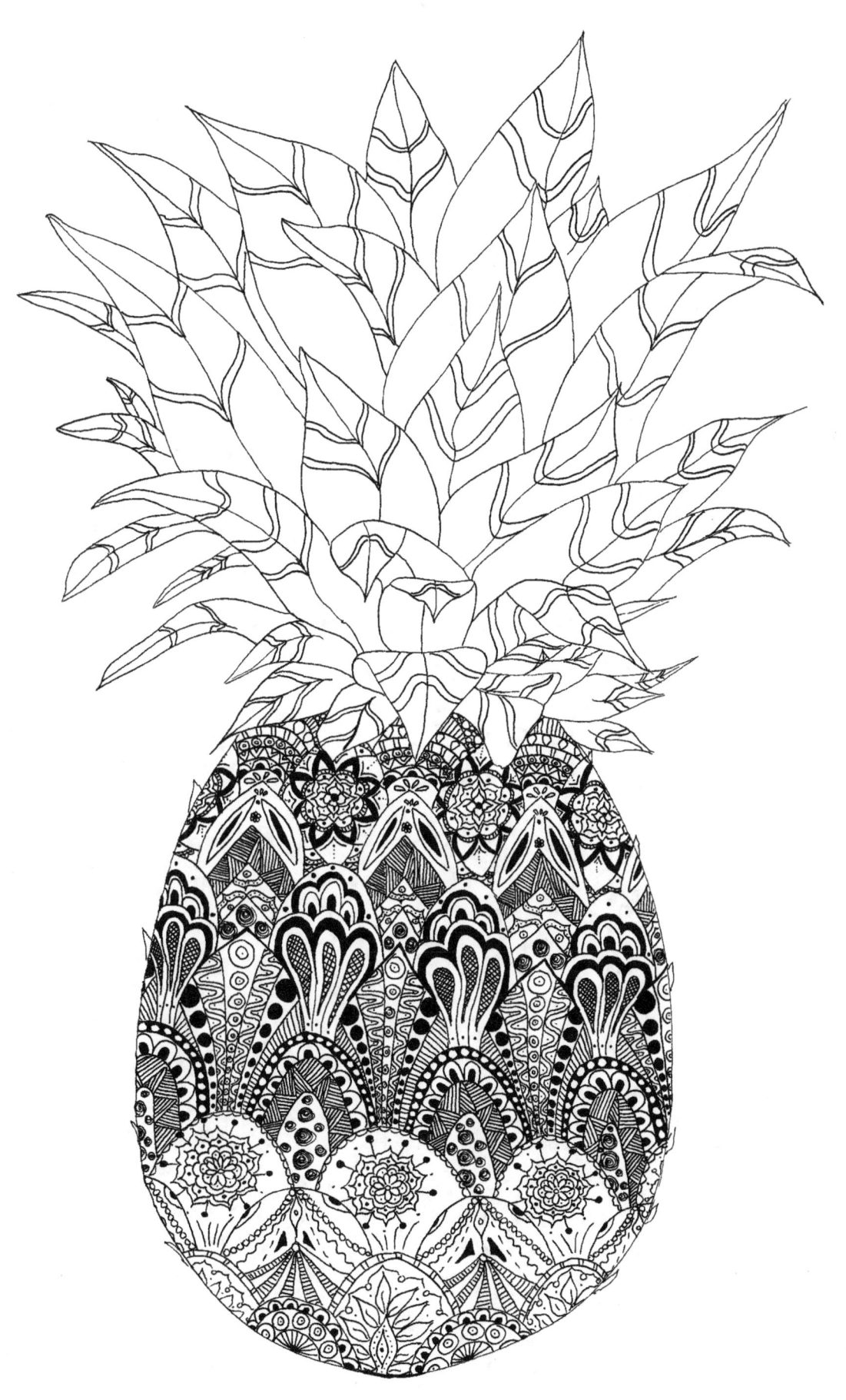

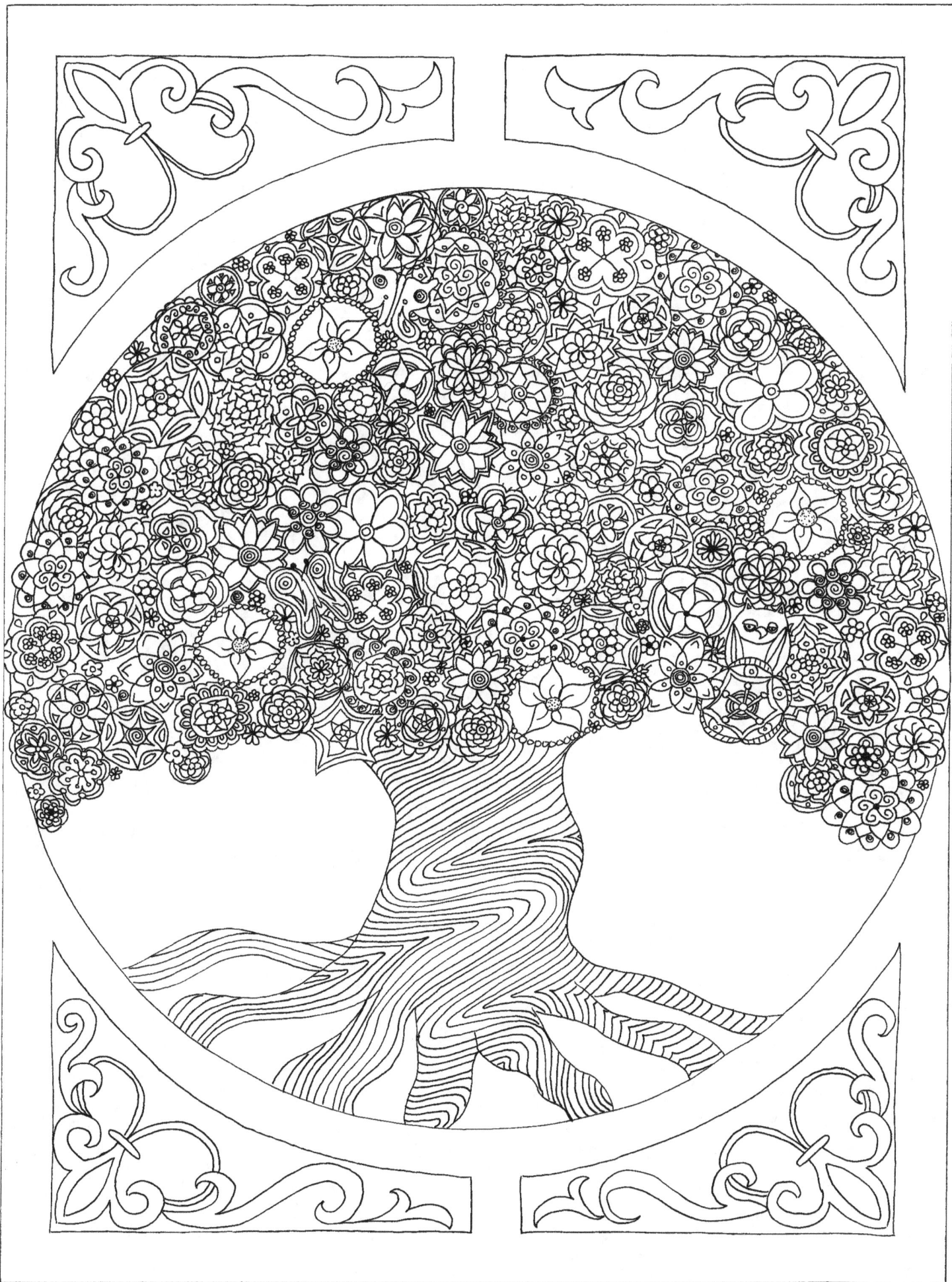

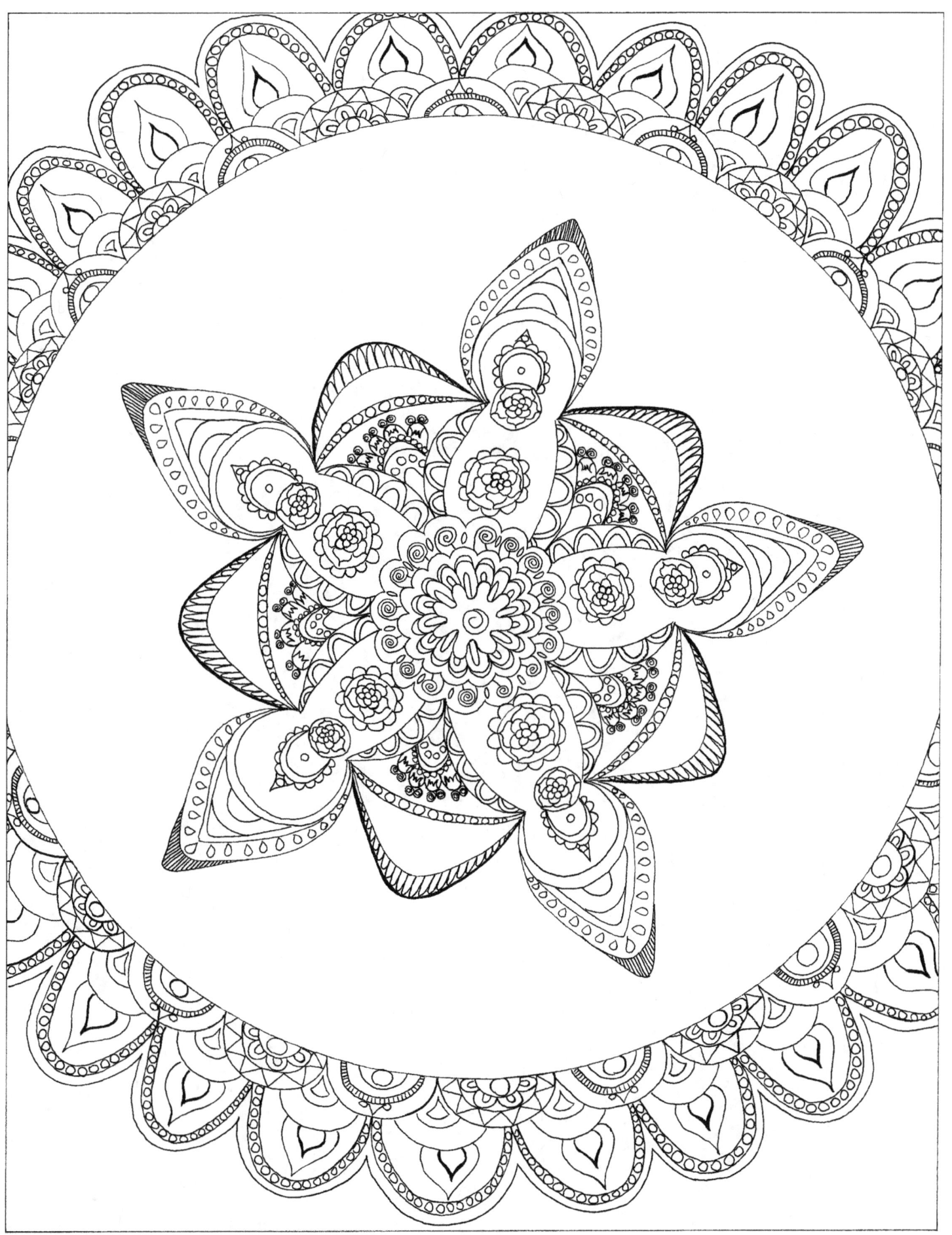

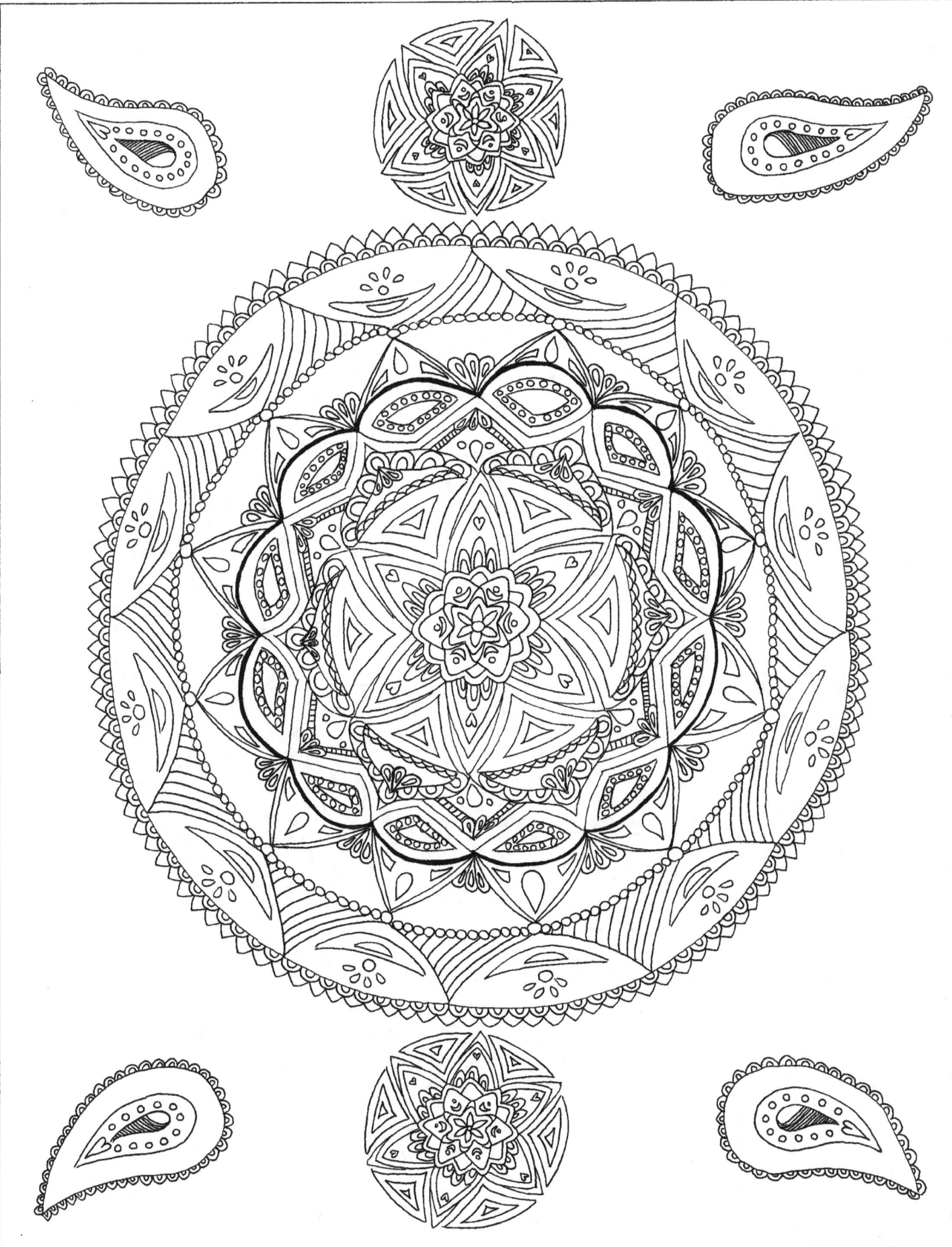

Chapter 7
Creative Rosalien

Norway

Facebook : Creative Rosalien

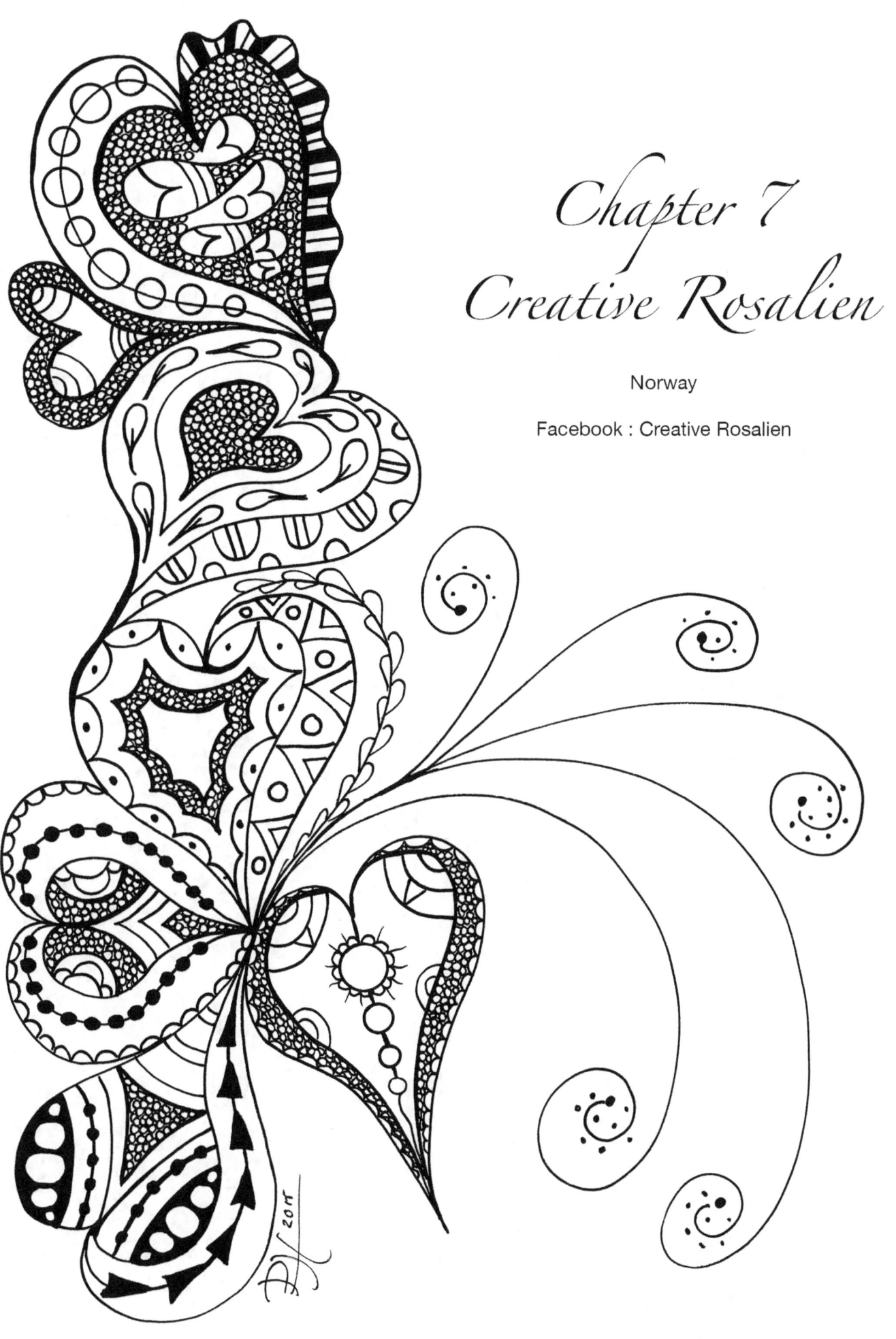

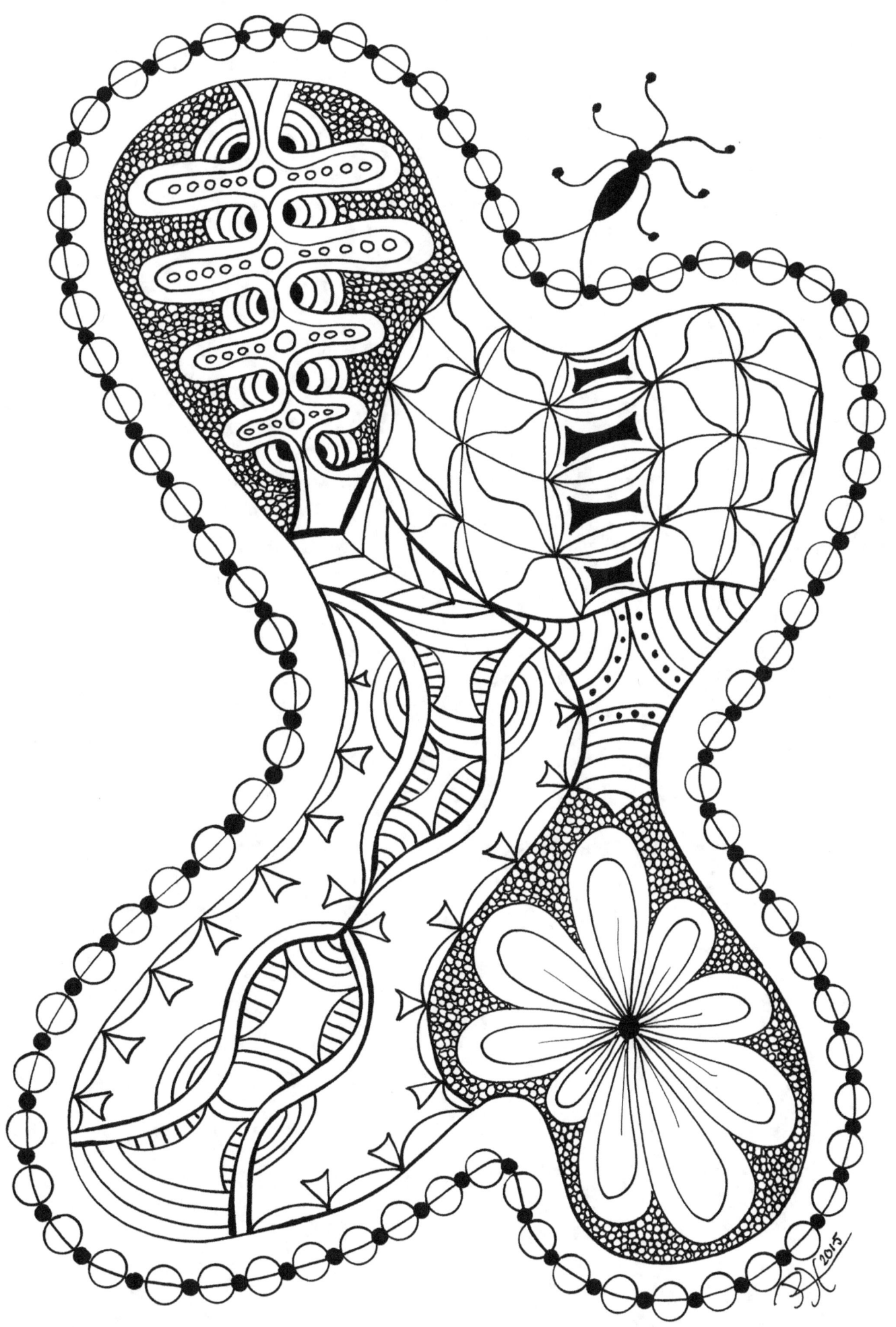

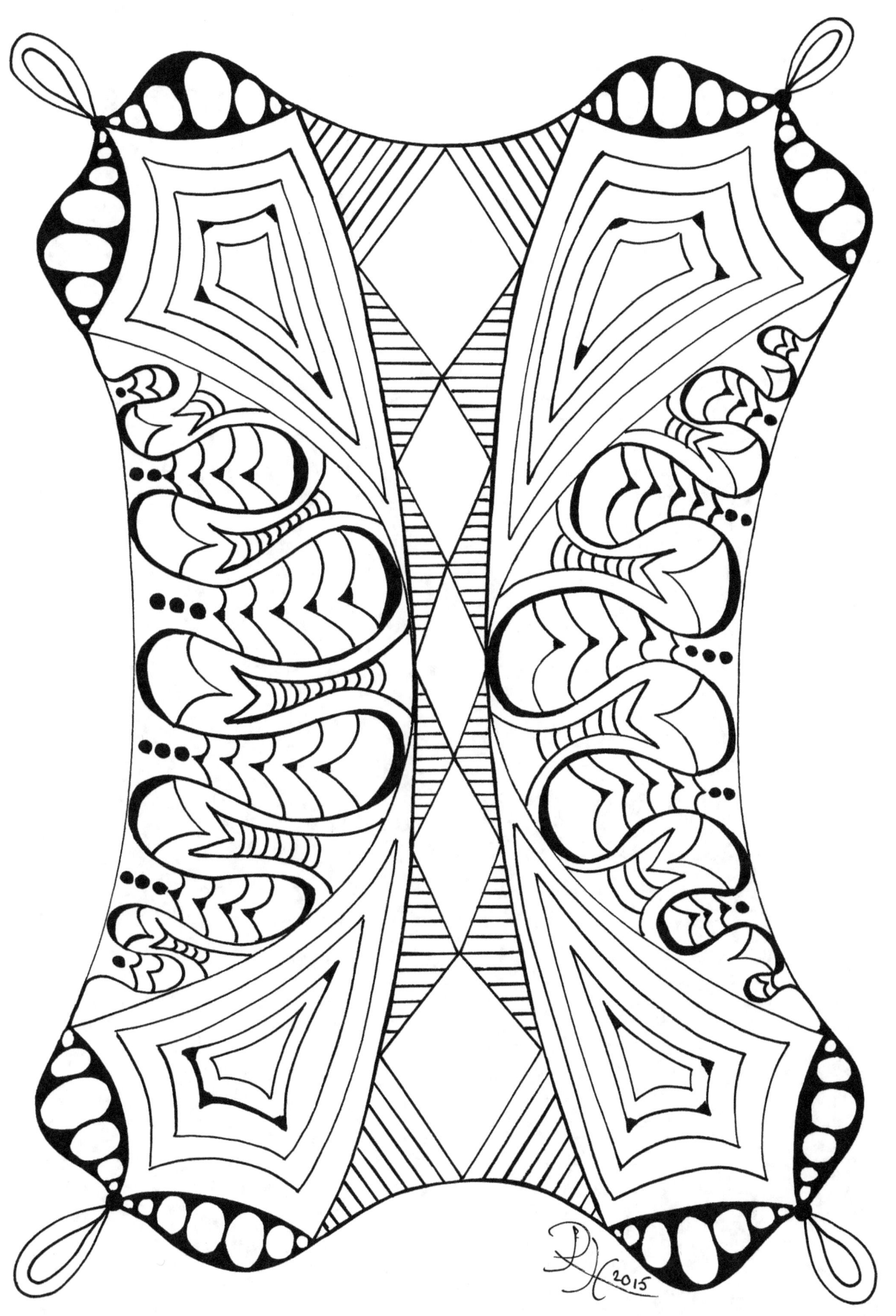

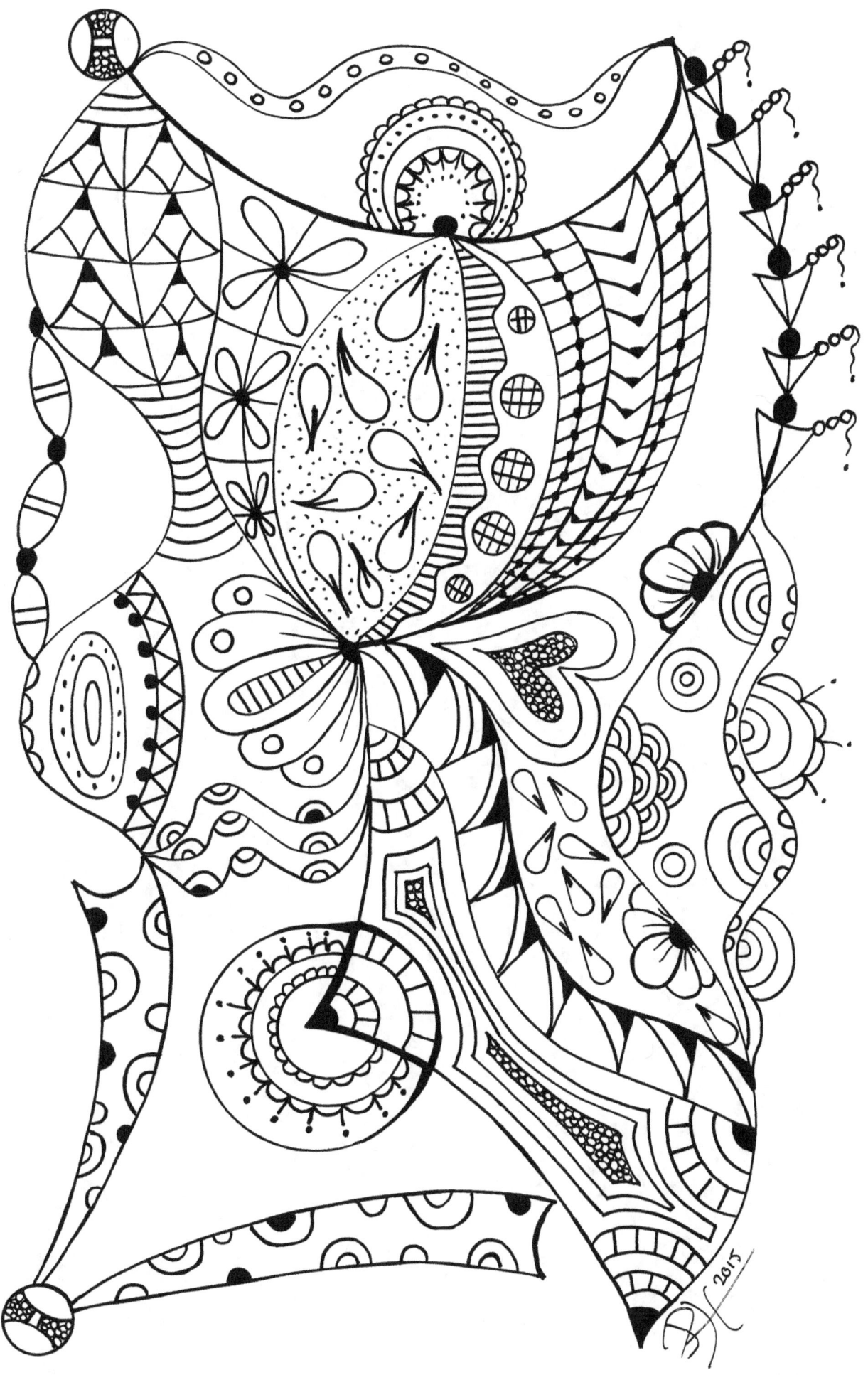

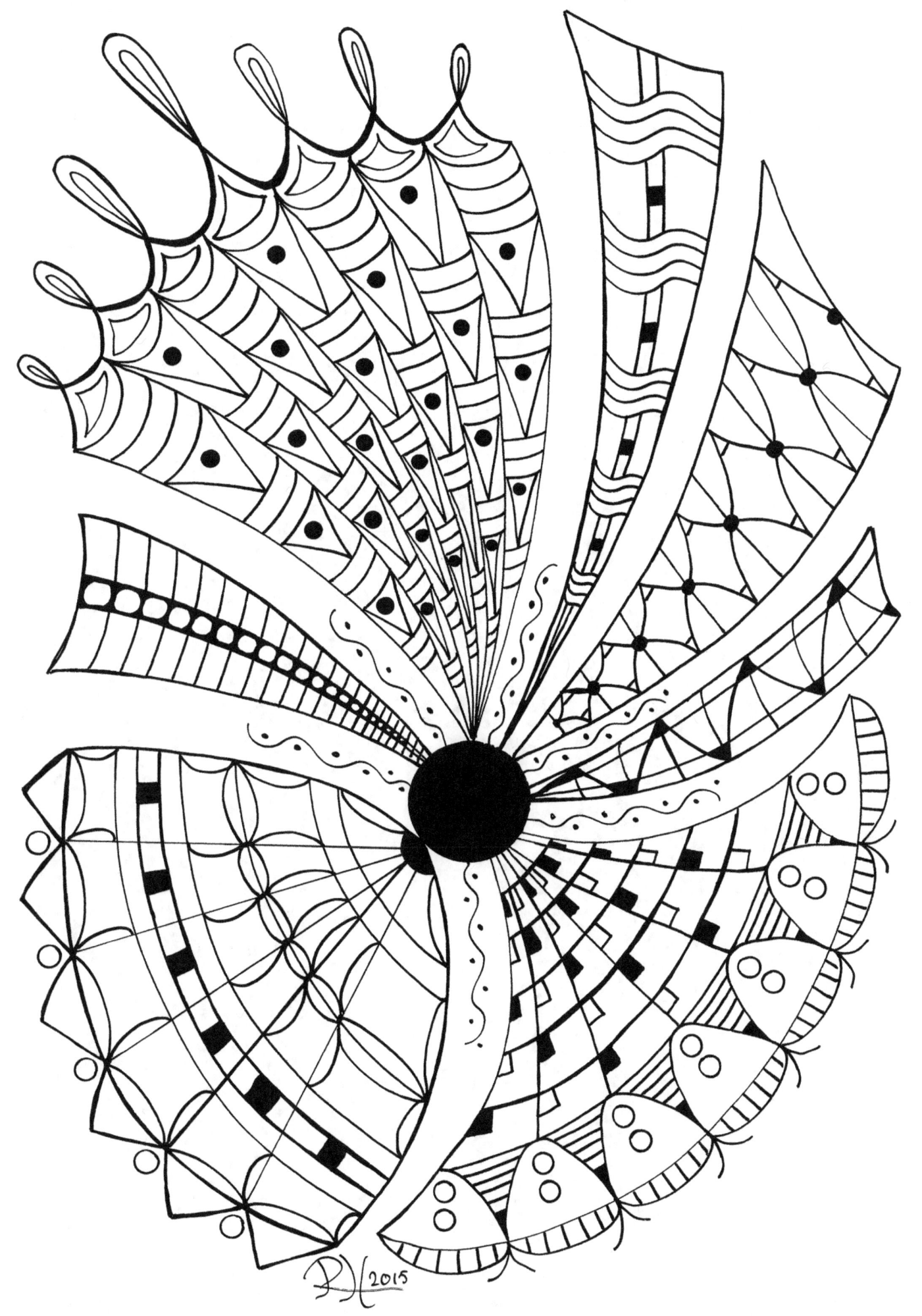

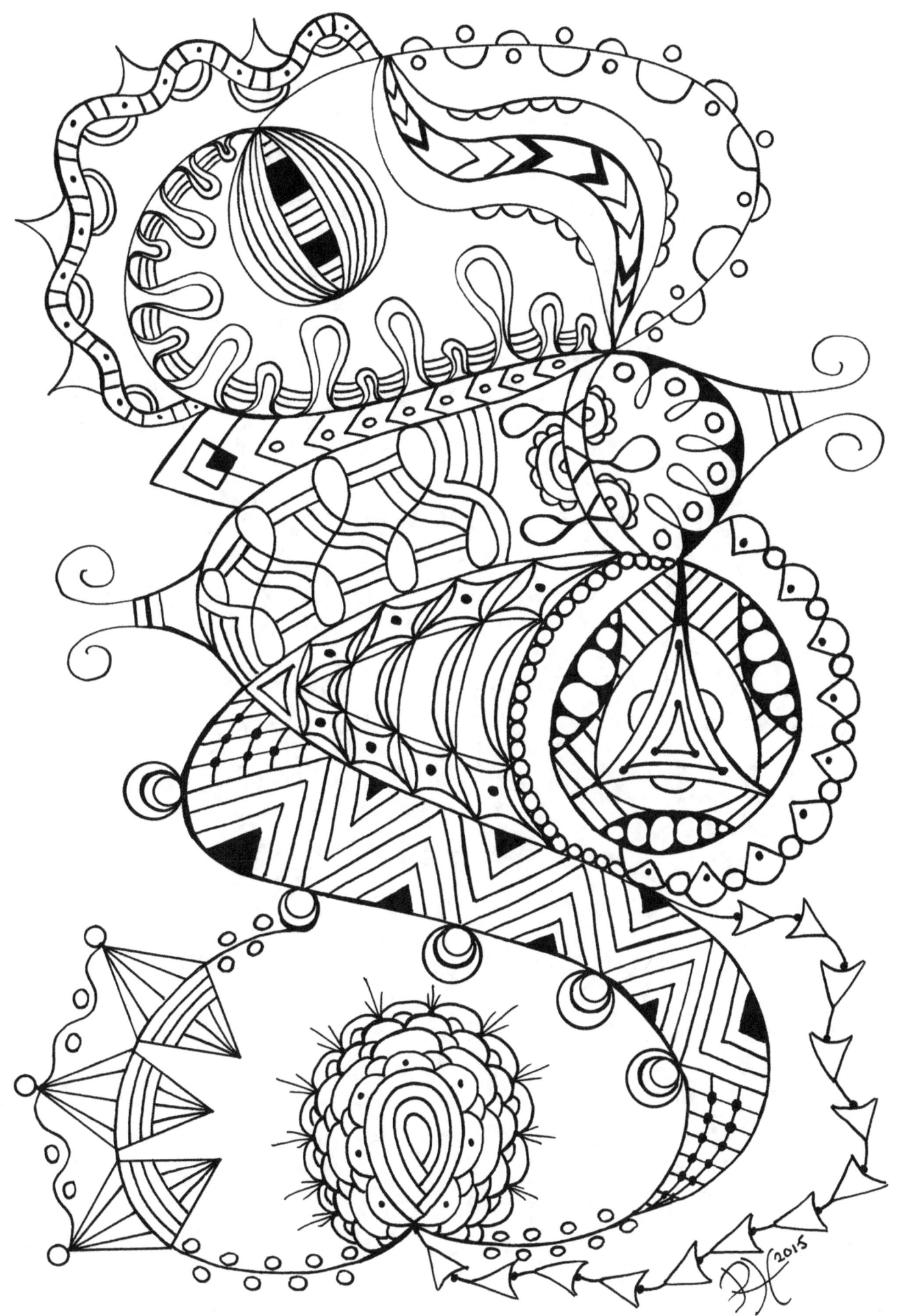

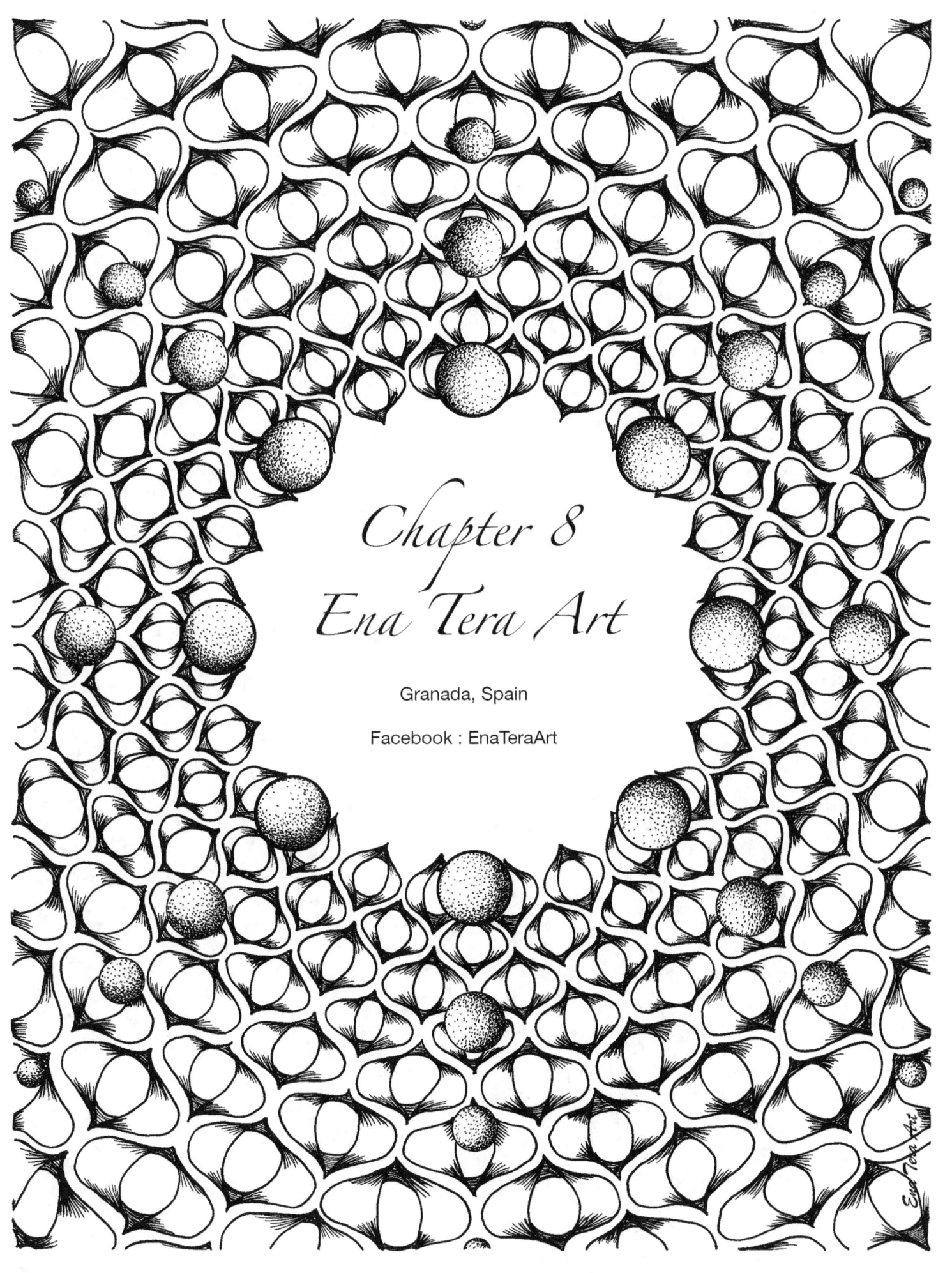

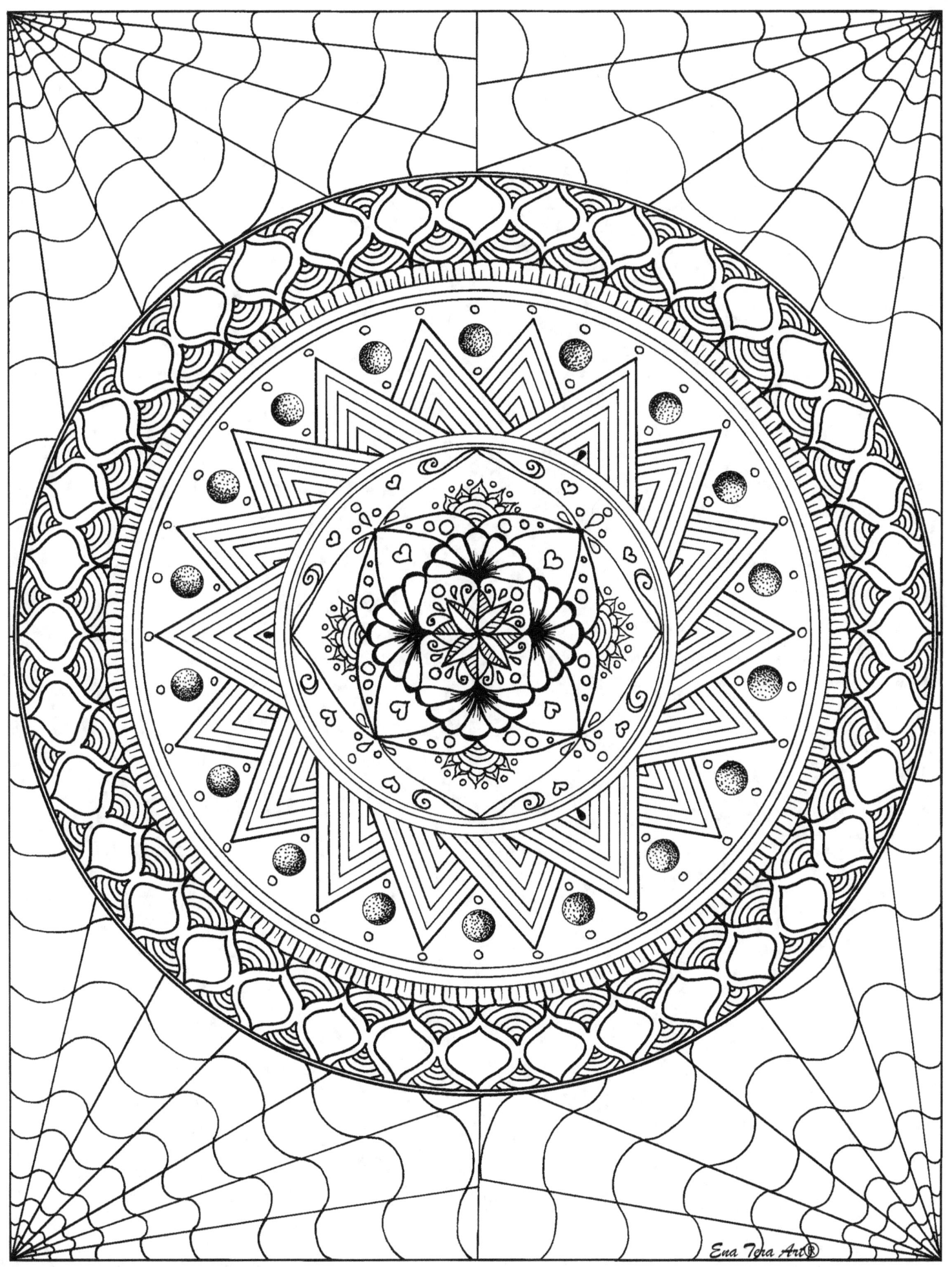

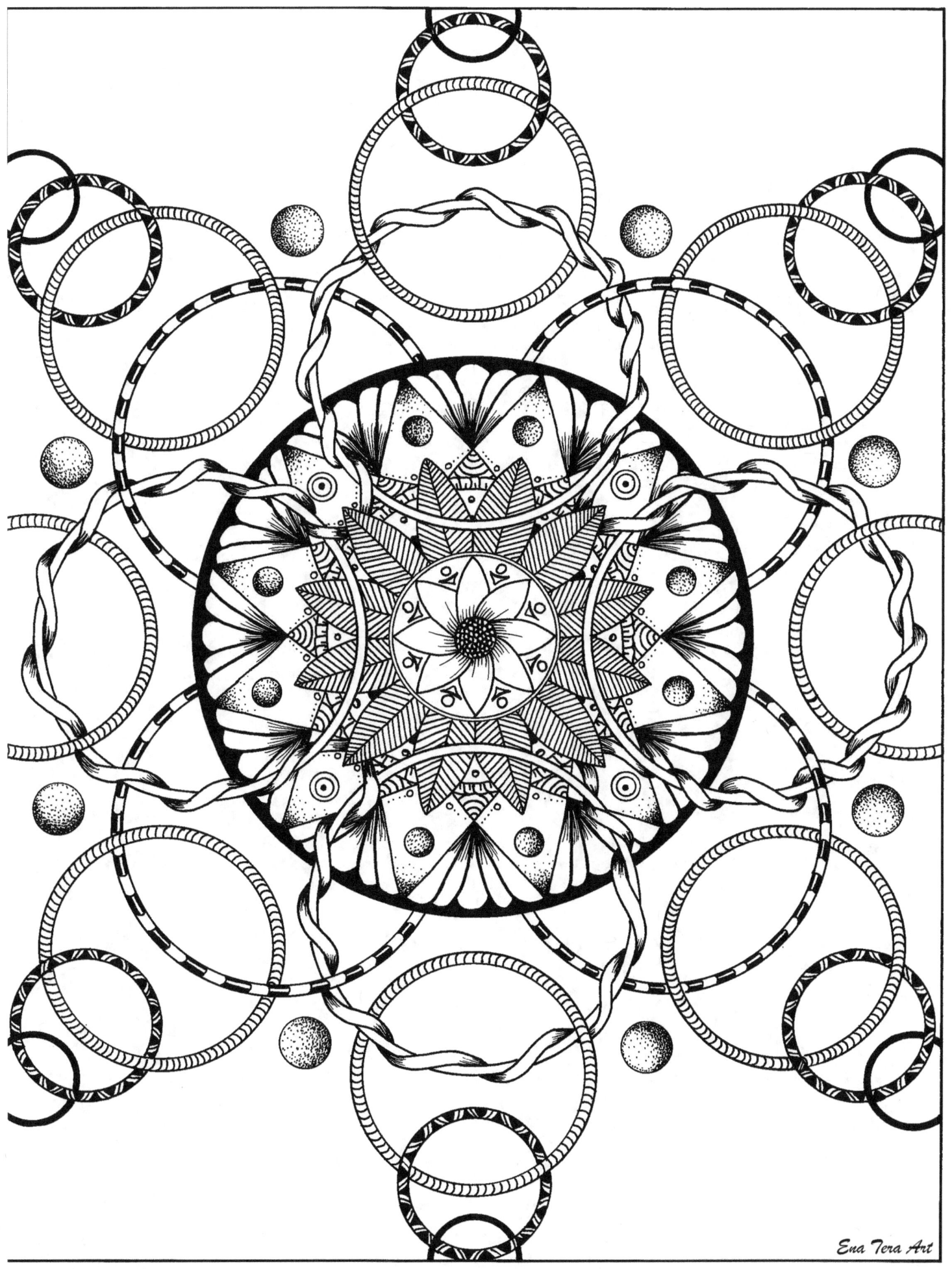

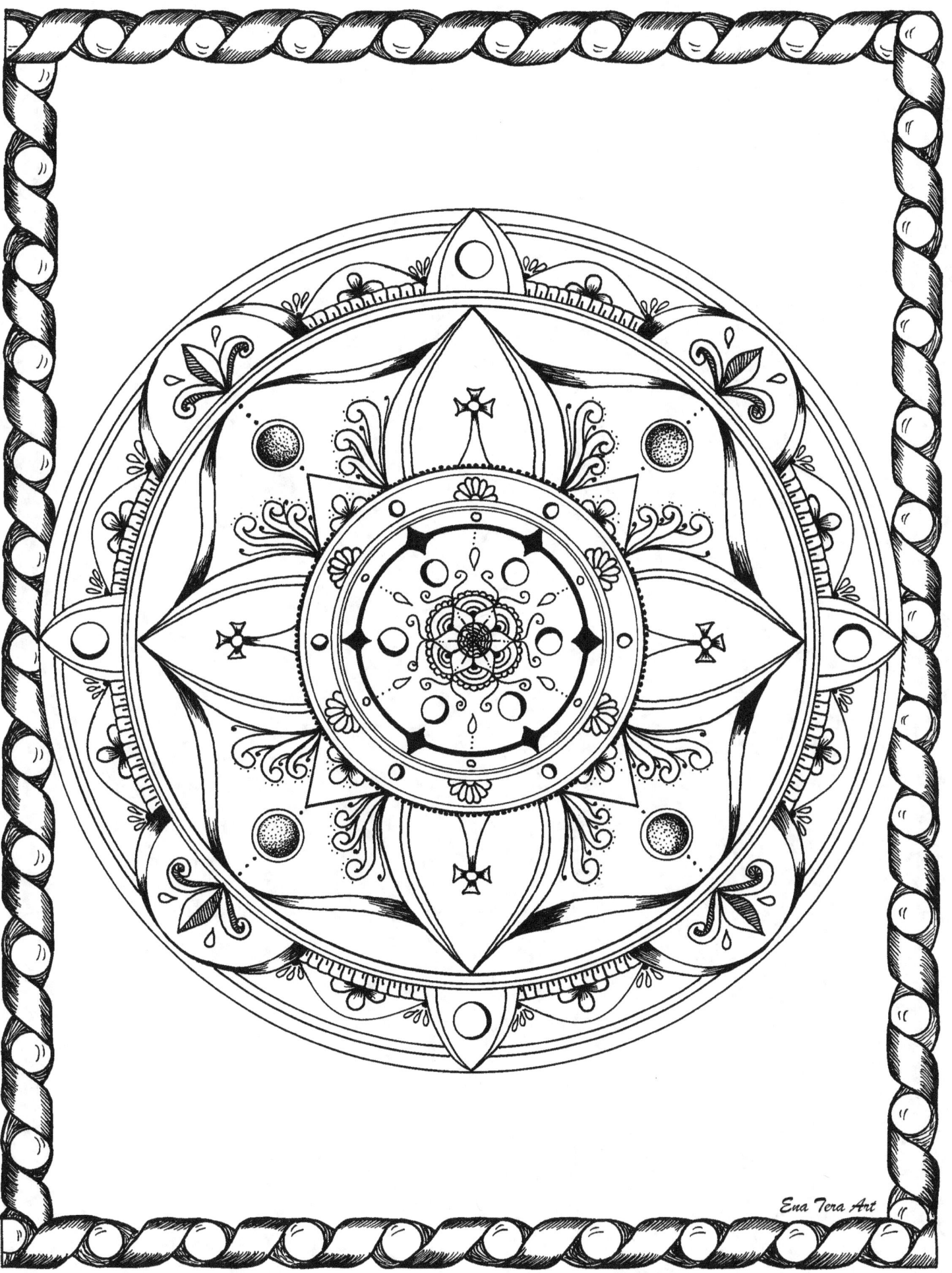

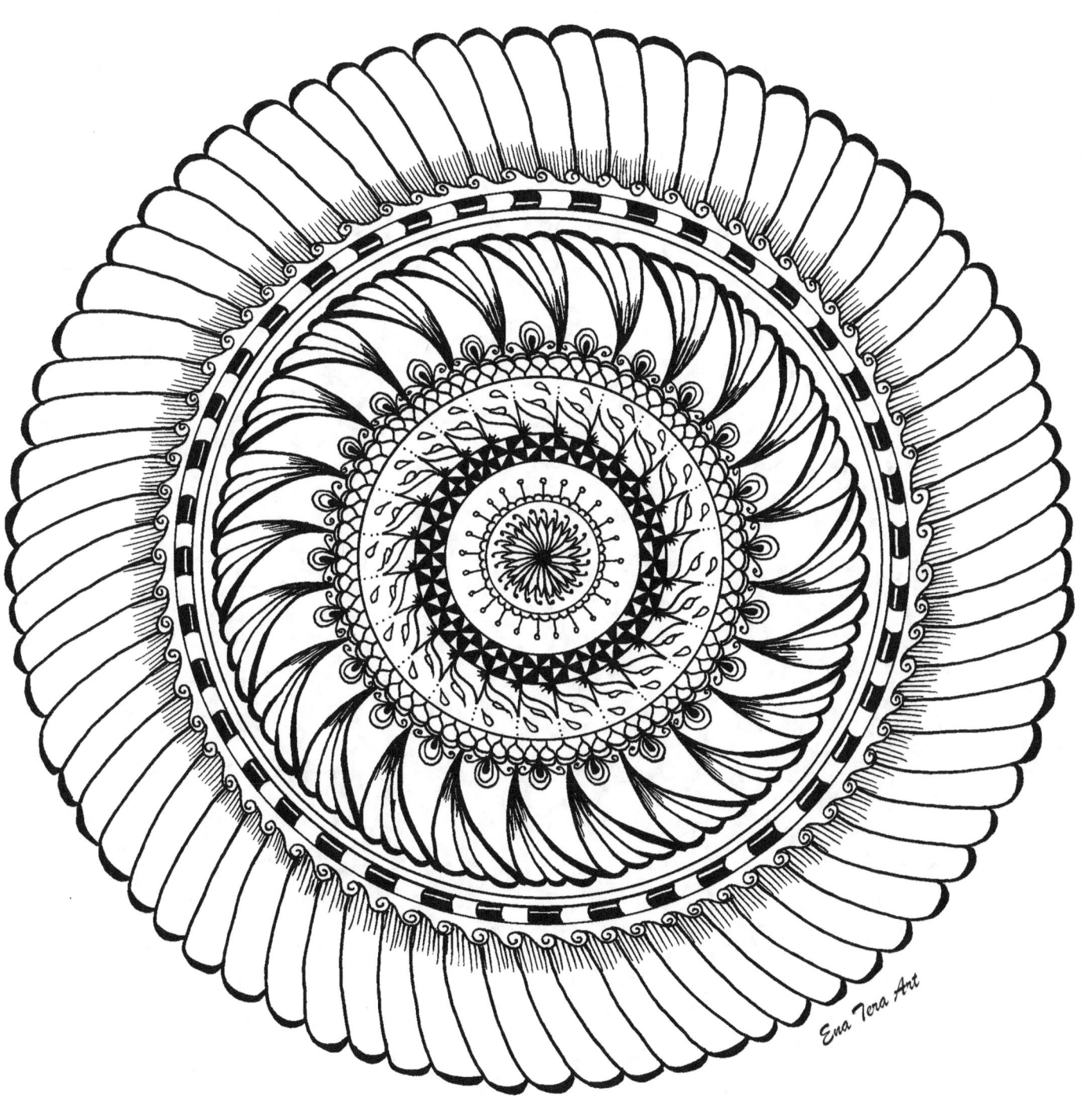

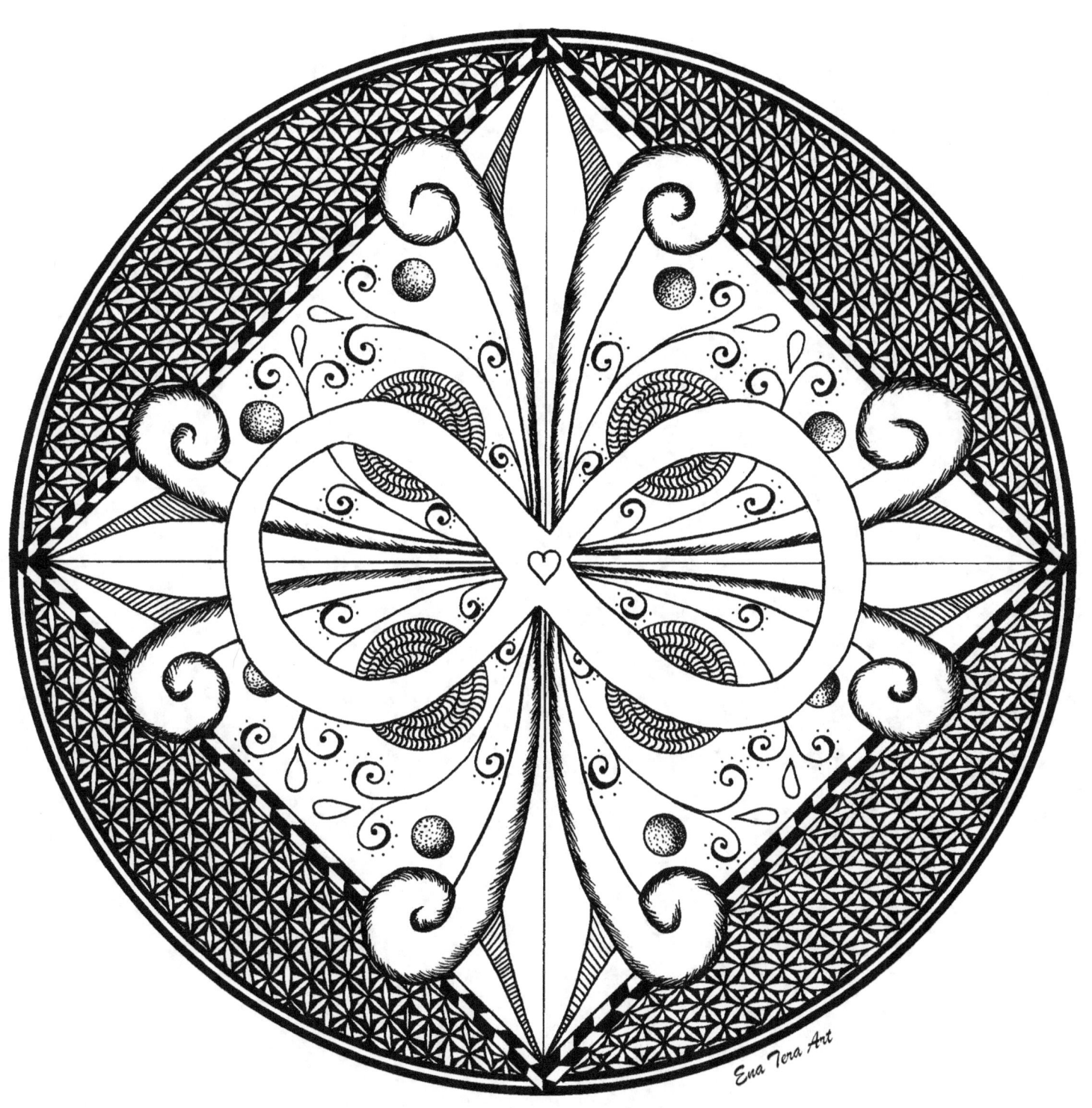

Chapter 9
Esther Lafiebre
Canarias, Spain

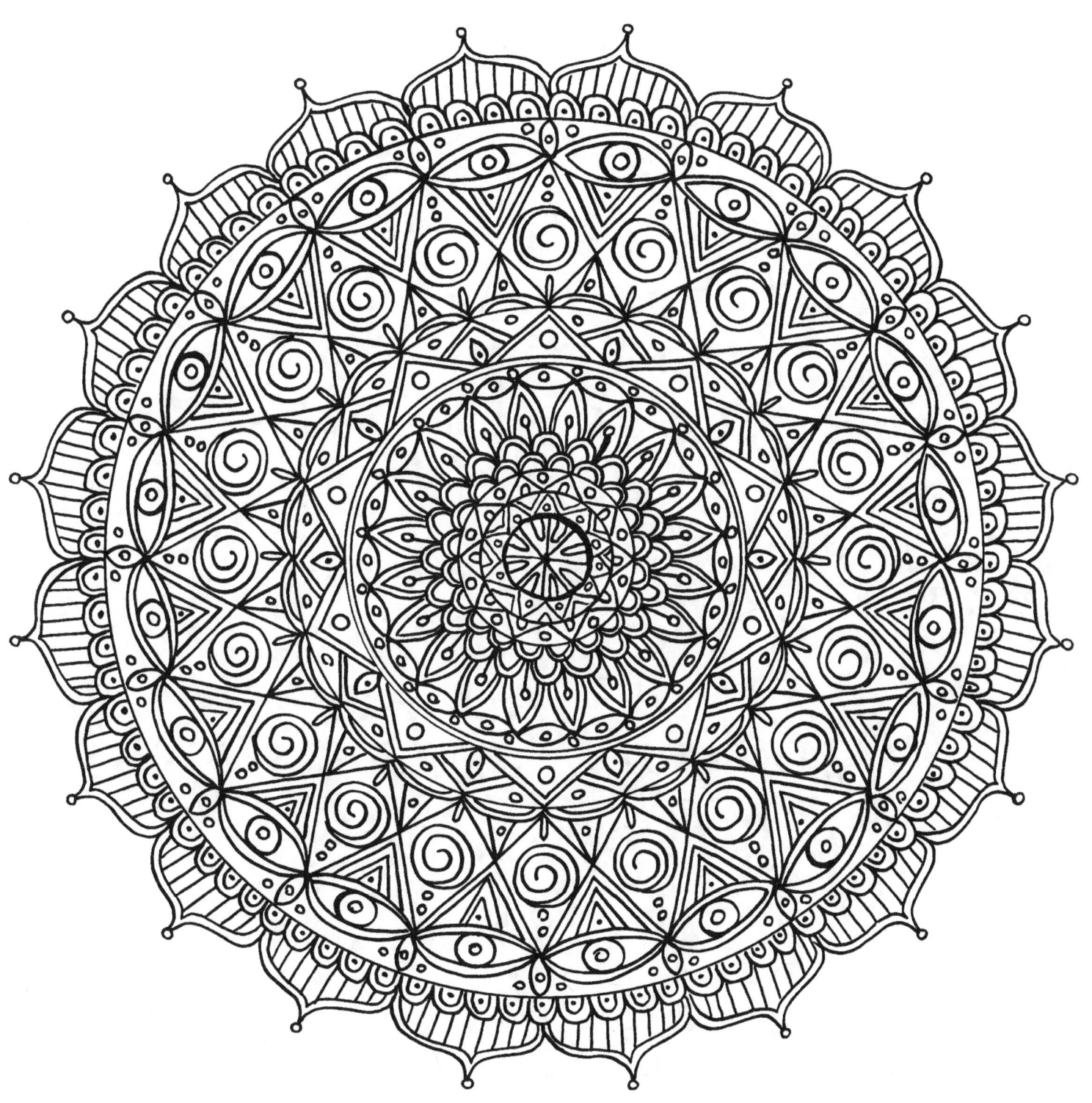

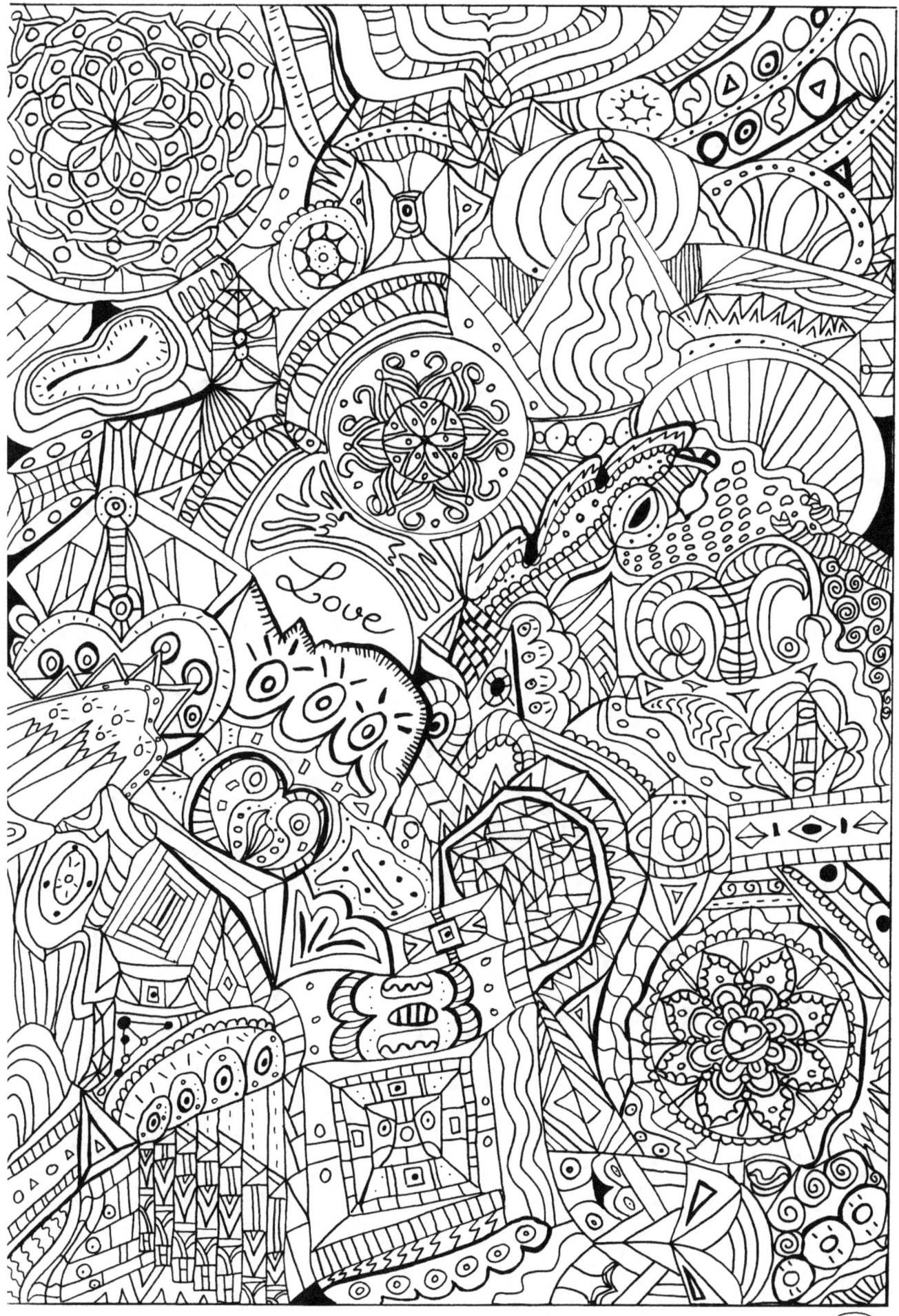

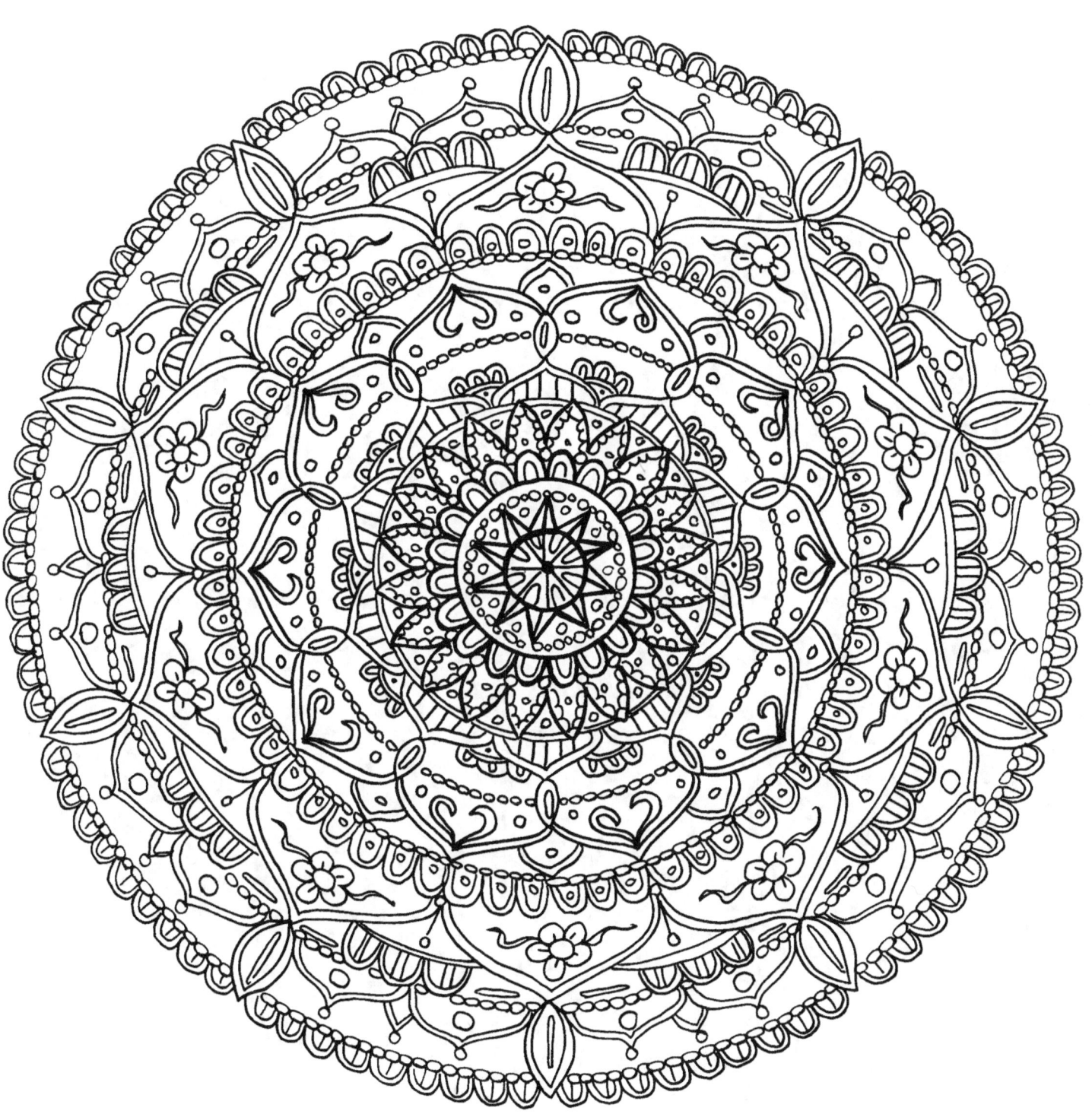

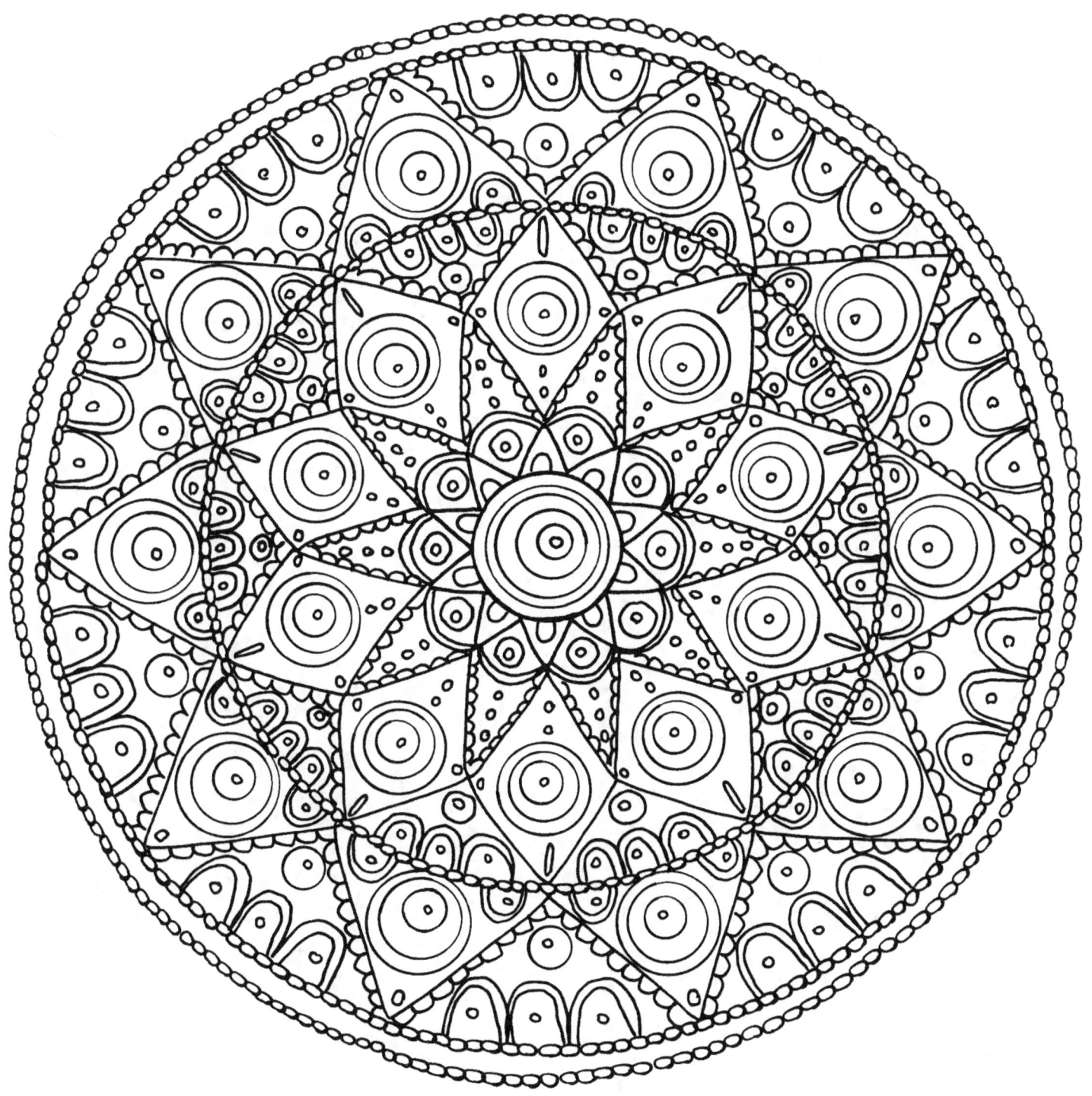

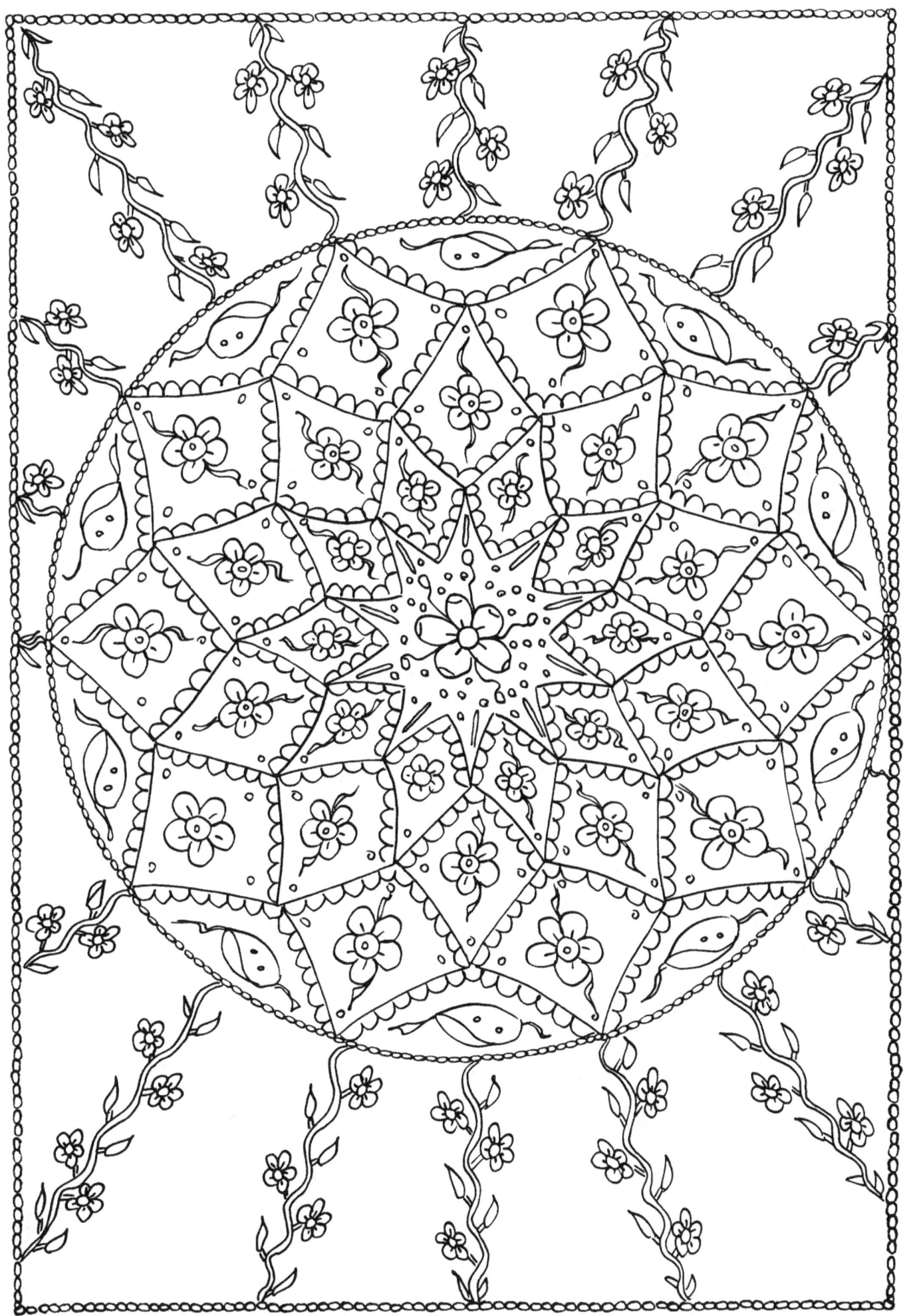

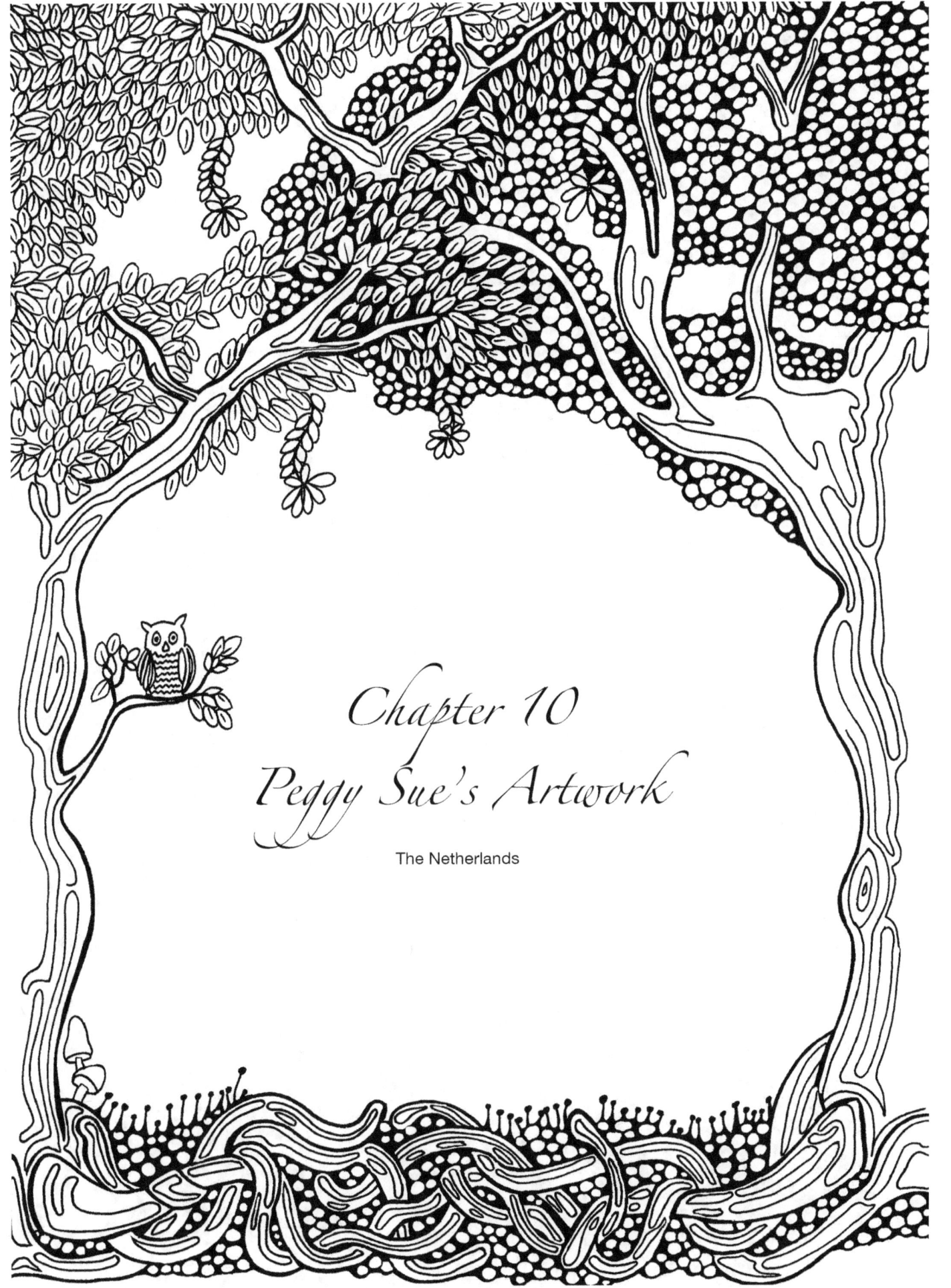

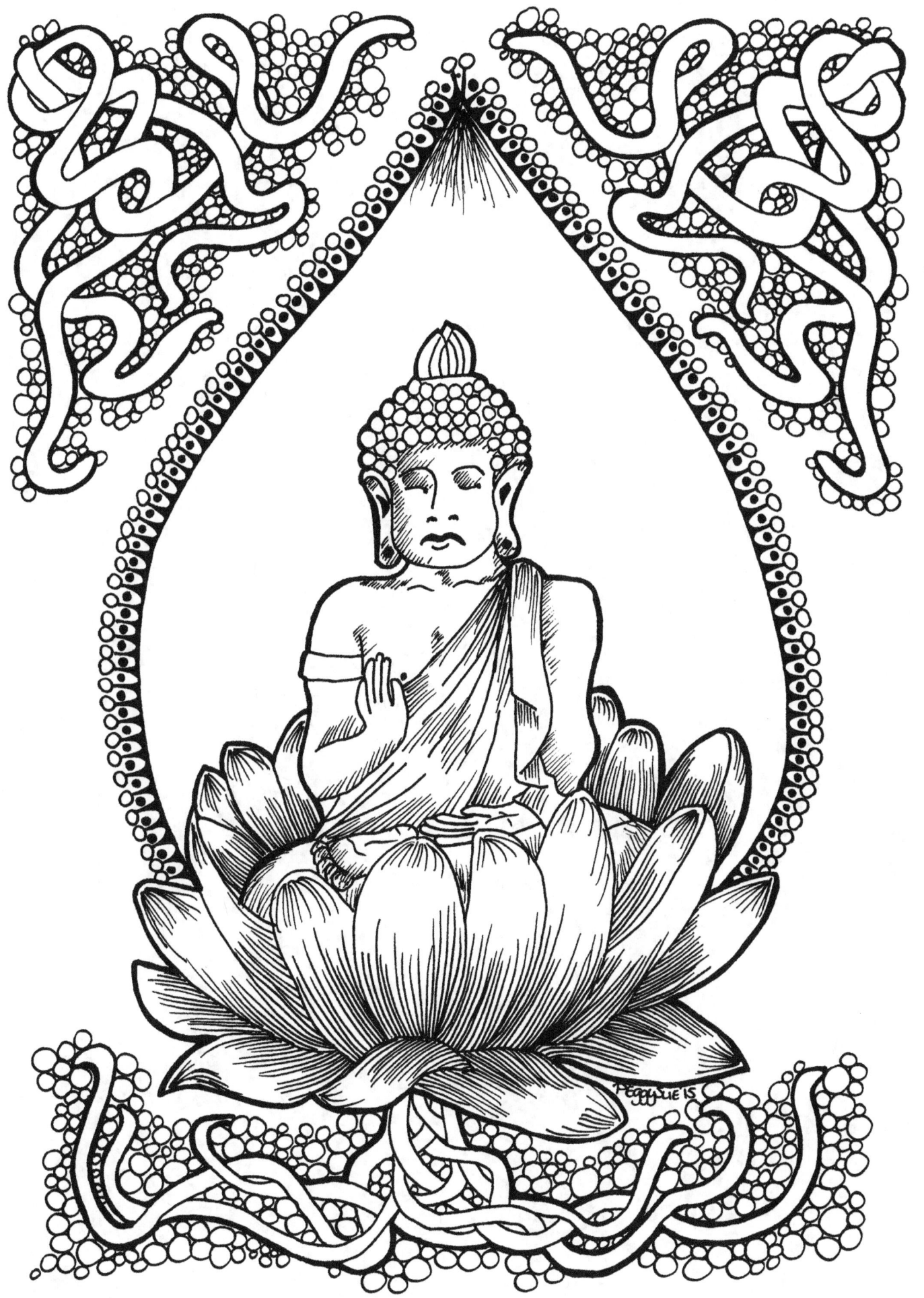

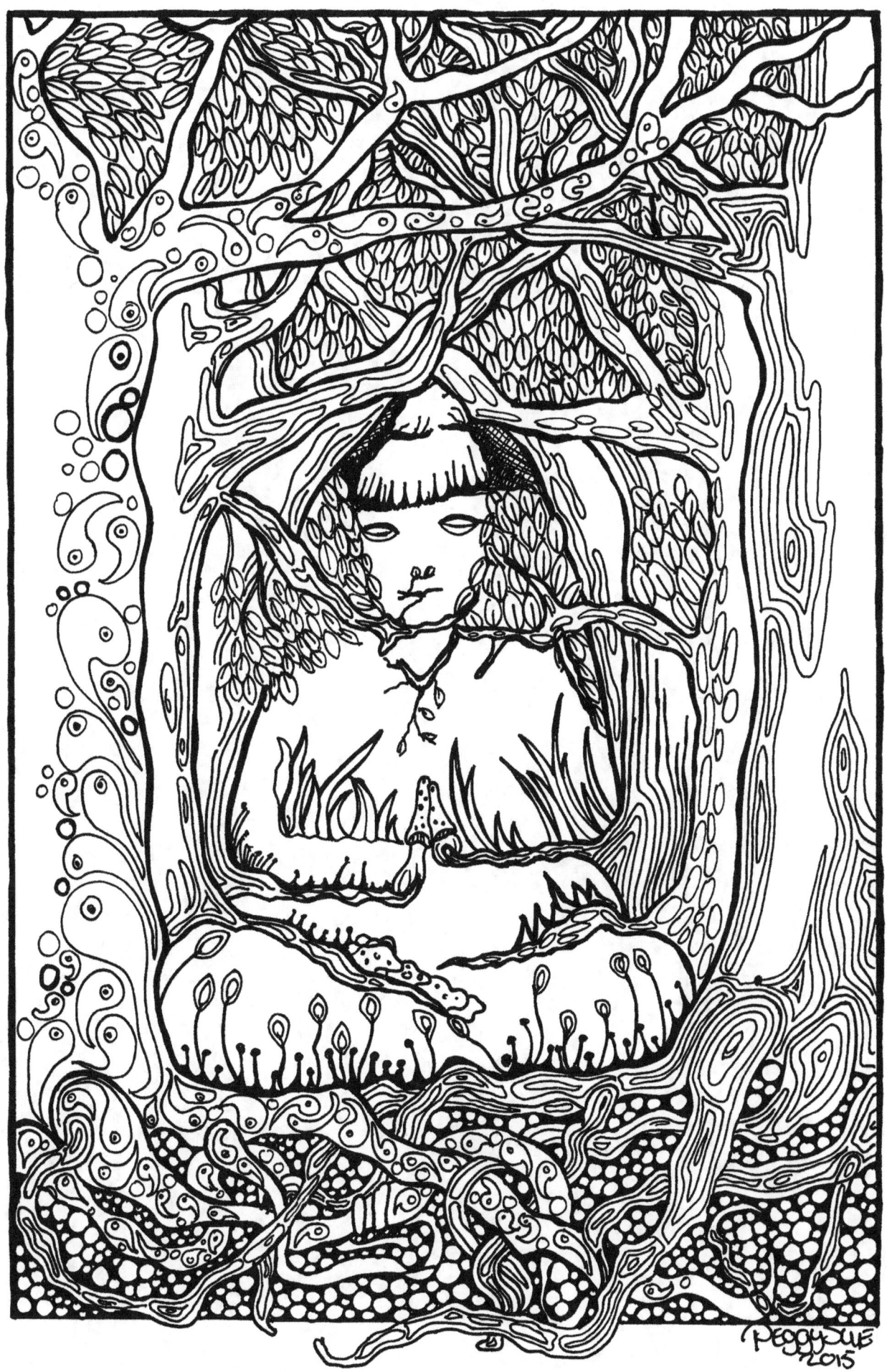

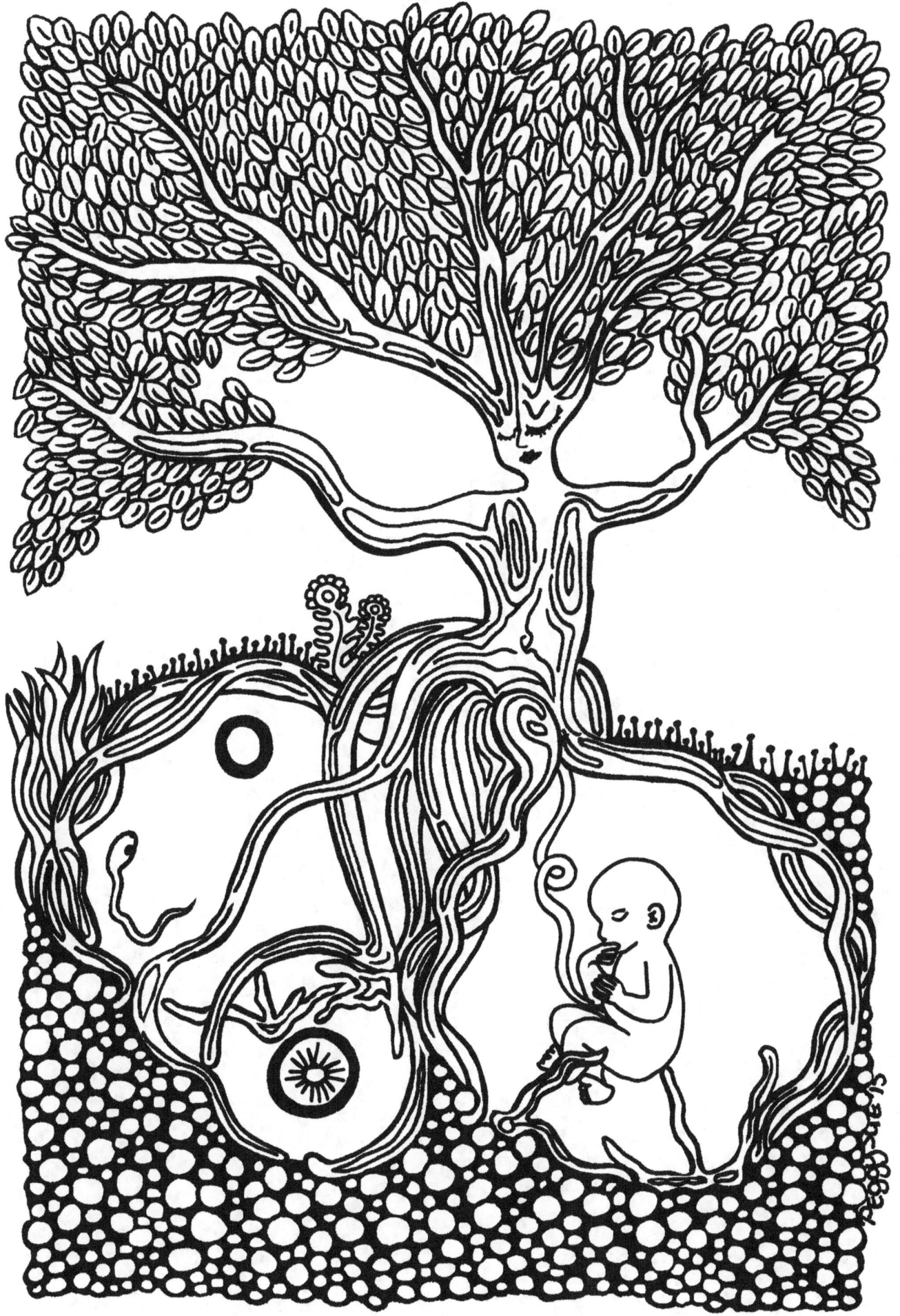

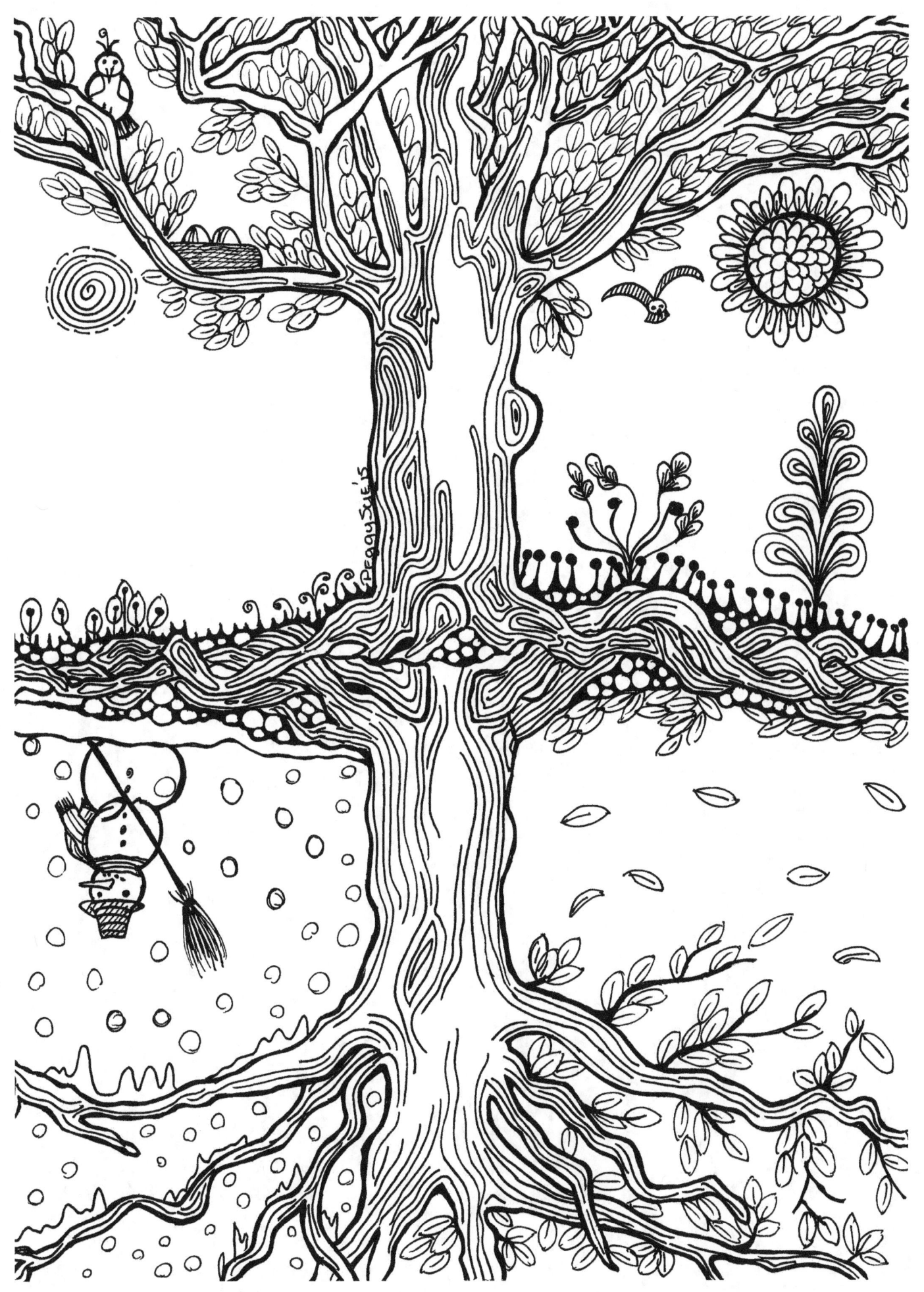

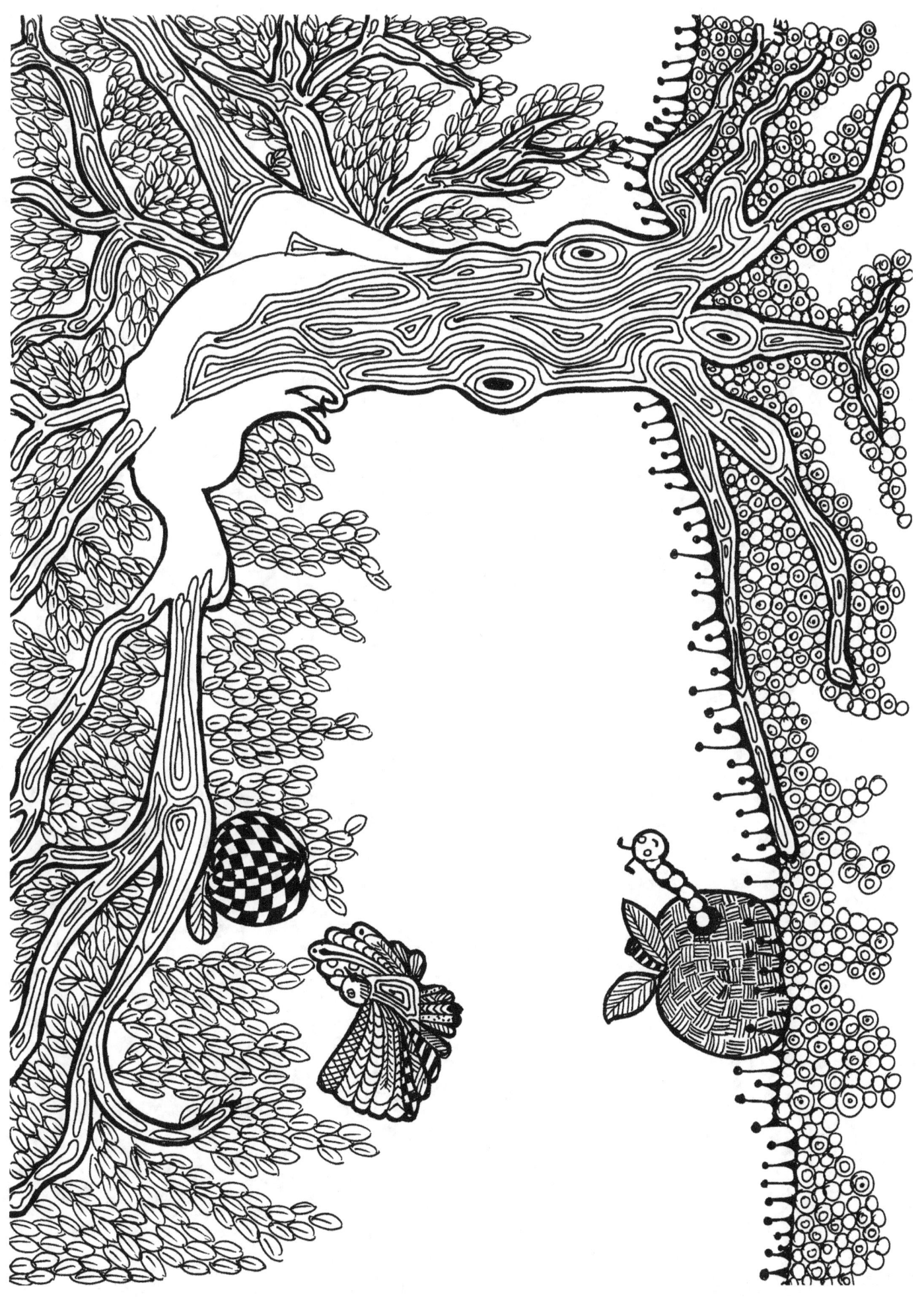

We from Global Doodle Gems, hope your journey through our book has been a pleasant one!

Please feel free to share your colored versions with us here:

https://www.facebook.com/groups/globaldoodlegems/

In our group you can meet the artists and enjoy exclusive freebies, video previews and participate in our community charity books "100 Doodles from 100 Doodlers" and so much more…. if you are wishing, that you could have the Chapter pages without the text, well then swing on by the group and get them for free in the freebie pdf for volume 7……

Are you curious about Volume 8?....well, just take a look at the next 2 pages and you will know what to exspect in the next volume of "Global Doodle Gems"!

"Global Doodle Gems" Volume 8 Preview

Les galaxies de 'Qi

Marie-Eve Klein

Irena Sergeeva

Nicole Whelan

L'aety Esperanza

Jane Levi

Johanna Ans

Asma Zergui

Fafahé

Mia Pelletier

Meet the artists feautured in "GDG" Volume 8

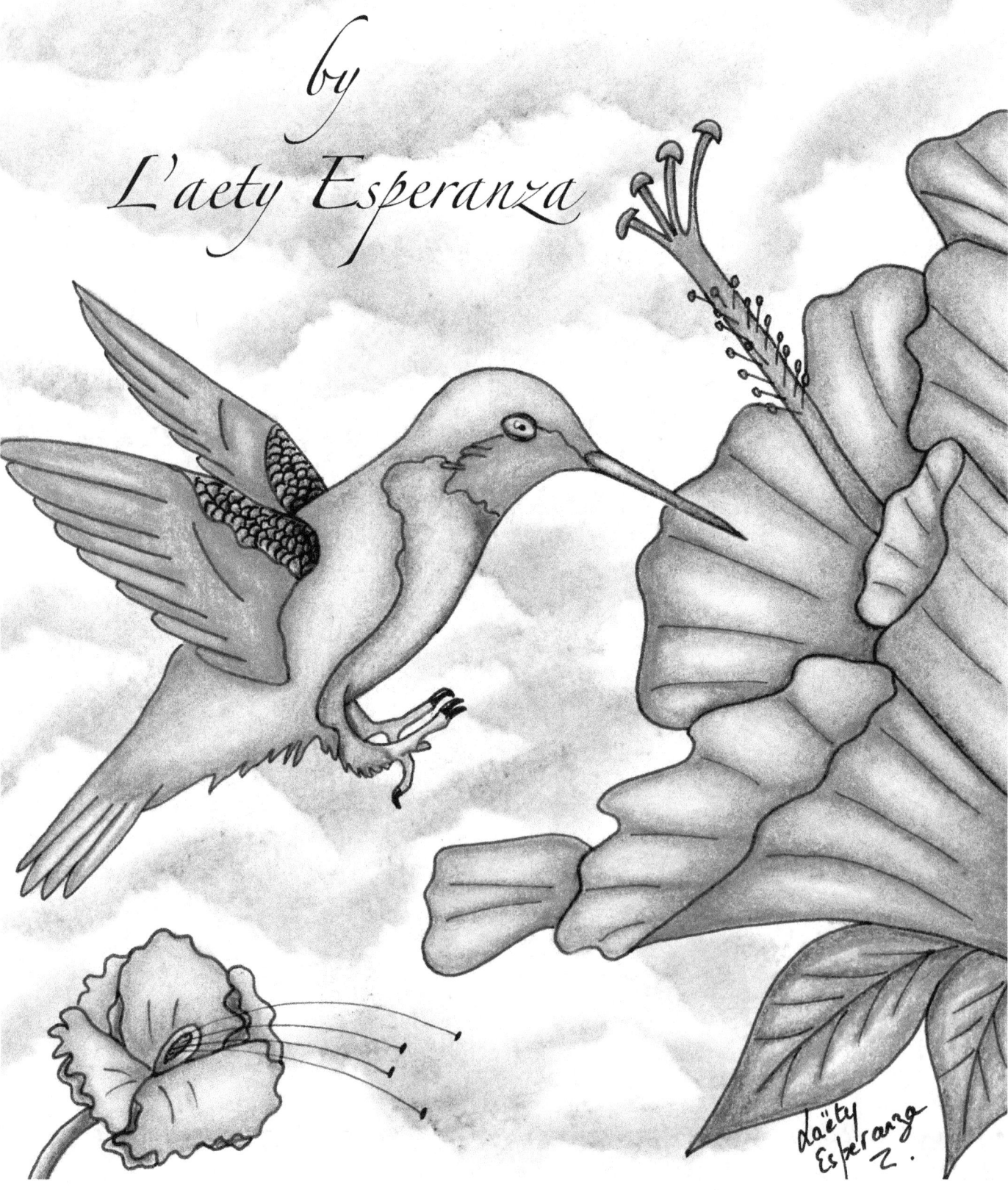

www.ingramcontent.com/pod-product-compliance
Lightning Source LLC
Chambersburg PA
CBHW082208220526
45470CB00010B/3083